T0305764

# THE SUBPRIME CRISIS

Lessons for
Business Students

# THE SUBPRIME CRISIS

## Lessons for Business Students

Jaime Luque

University of Wisconsin-Madison, USA

**W**⊖ **World Scientific**

NEW JERSEY · LONDON · SINGAPORE · BEIJING · SHANGHAI · HONG KONG · TAIPEI · CHENNAI · TOKYO

*Published by*

World Scientific Publishing Co. Pte. Ltd.

5 Toh Tuck Link, Singapore 596224

*USA office:* 27 Warren Street, Suite 401-402, Hackensack, NJ 07601

*UK office:* 57 Shelton Street, Covent Garden, London WC2H 9HE

**Library of Congress Cataloging-in-Publication Data**

Names: Luque, Jaime, 1981–    author.

Title: The subprime crisis : lessons for business students / Jaime P. Luque
   (University of Wisconsin-Madison, USA).

Description: New Jersey : World Scientific, [2017] | Includes bibliographical references and index.

Identifiers: LCCN 2016041701 | ISBN 9789813200036 (hc : alk. paper)

Subjects: LCSH: Global Financial Crisis, 2008–2009. | Subprime mortgage loans--United States. |
   Recessions--United States--History--21st century. |
   Financial crises--United States--History--21st century.

Classification: LCC HB3717 2008 .L87 2017 | DDC 330.973/0931--dc23

LC record available at https://lccn.loc.gov/2016041701

**British Library Cataloguing-in-Publication Data**

A catalogue record for this book is available from the British Library.

Desk Editors: Suraj Kumar/Philly Lim

Typeset by Stallion Press
Email: enquiries@stallionpress.com

Printed in Singapore

# Dedication

This book would not have been possible without the numerous contributions of students who took my "Regional and urban economics" course at the University of Wisconsin — Madison. To them I dedicate this book.

# Preface

*In collaboration with* Eduardo De La Torre

The first major global economic contraction of the 21st century, or the "Great Recession," as it is more commonly known, began in December 2007, and would prove to be one of the most catastrophic economic events in postmodern history. The bursting of the American housing bubble and the subprime mortgage crisis that followed are widely attributed as being the primary causes for this economic downturn. This crisis metastasized to numerous sectors of the economy, and its effects were disastrous for millions of Americans. An event of this magnitude elicits two natural questions: How did the economy get to this point, and how can we prevent this from happening again?

The subprime mortgage crisis stemmed in large part from an earlier subprime credit expansion that occurred in the early 2000s. To mitigate the minor recession caused by plummeting Internet and technology stocks that were previously overvalued during the "dot com boom," the Federal Reserve responded by slashing interest rates to 1 percent. These low-interest rates directly translated to consumers as a lower cost of borrowing, and they responded to this incentive by increasing homeownership rates.

As demand for houses increased, so did their price, providing a lucrative opportunity for mortgage companies. Mortgage companies responded with an expansion of subprime mortgage loans; in other words, high-risk borrowers faced less underwriting scrutiny when applying for credit. These subprime loans often had low initial teaser rates, and higher adjustable rates that would kick in later. Due to the sophisticated nature of these loans, some home buyers did not even fully understand the kind of loans they were getting into.

In response to increasing home prices, consumers developed an irrational expectation of an always expanding housing market. Although home prices were rising, house sales kept increasing as well due to consumers' belief that prices would continue to rise, creating incentives for people to purchase homes as investments. Home buyers often overlooked basic decision-making signals when buying homes in exchange for the prospect of a future profit.

This "subprime market" for credit expanded quickly, and developments in loan securitization made it easy for lenders to sell these mortgages in the secondary mortgage market. These mortgages were later repacked into mortgage-backed securities (MBS) that diversified the risk of these toxic assets and presented them as healthy investment vehicles. The creation of these financial instruments undermined the responsibility lenders have in awarding loans, as banks did not internalize the risk associated with the subprime mortgages they were approving and they took an "originate to sell" approach. Securitized subprime mortgage debts were purchased by prestigious firms such as Goldman Sachs and Lehman Brothers. Meanwhile, credit rating agencies had no problem giving these collateralized debt obligations the highest credit ratings, despite the fact that the underlying assets were risky and toxic. In essence, mortgage originating banks were able to hide their exposure by selling mortgages in the secondary market.

This credit expansion *vis-à-vis* risky subprime lending continued uninterrupted until 2006, when a large amount of consumers started defaulting on their loans. Foreclosures became widespread, partially because consumers were granted predatory loans that they were not able to maintain payments on after the initial teaser interest rate expired. These foreclosures in turn caused a widespread decline in housing prices. For the first time in decades, home prices were falling, and consumer confidence in the housing sector began to deteriorate.

An important consequence of the steep increase in the mortgage default rate was that banks and financial institutions had to face huge losses. Specifically, mortgage lenders felt the blow more directly. An example of such is New Century Financial, which was an industry leader in subprime mortgage origination. It was forced to file for bankruptcy as a result of financial underperformance and severe liquidity problems. While New Century Financial was the biggest of the mortgage lenders to falter, it was not alone in that regard; numerous other mortgage lenders were forced to close as well.

Investment banks were also heavily affected by the subprime mortgage crisis. Bear Stearns, the fifth largest investment bank at the time, was subsequently rescued in 2008 by the government. The Federal Reserve basically provided JP Morgan Chase with enough money to be able to lend to Bear Stearns through purchasing a chunk of its assets in order to keep it afloat. Ultimately, Bear Stearns was sold to JP Morgan Chase at a fire sale price, and became defunct as its own entity. In a similar manner, Merrill Lynch was purchased by Bank of America. Lehman Brothers, another leading investment bank, was forced to close its doors after failing.

Insurance companies were utilized by investment banks who held MBS as hedging instruments to protect themselves from the risks they were incurring as a result of purchasing risky subprime debt bundles. Investment banks insured against the default of debt instruments, specifically MBS, through credit default swaps. When mortgage defaults started to become widespread, these insurance companies also took big hits. AIG, an insurance company that was a leader in credit default swaps, suffered catastrophic losses as a result. Things got so bad that the Federal Reserve had to intervene and bail out AIG, making it the largest government bailout of a private company in American history.

The two government sponsored enterprises that were at the forefront of providing subprime loans, Freddie Mac and Fannie

Mae had losses so huge that they were on the verge of not being able to operate. The federal government was forced to take over Freddie and Fannie as well in an attempt to contain a crumbling subprime mortgage market.

In order to combat what had become a widespread crisis, The Emergency Economic Stabilization Act of 2008 was signed into law by President George W. Bush. This authorized the federal government to spend 700 billion dollars to purchase toxic assets such as mortgage backed securities, as well as to provide liquidity to several banks. The rationale behind the bailout was that it was necessary to contain the economic crisis, to prevent the erosion of credit markets and to prevent an imminent economic depression. This decision to bail out the banks was extremely controversial, as this was the first time that the scope of government intervention in the economy was extended to such levels.

This begs the question — How did we get here? How did the subprime mortgage crisis originate? The answer is complicated but can be reduced down to at least four factors: (i) low-interest rates, which increased the demand for housing and in turn raised the prices of houses, (ii) the emergence and subsequent dominance of the "originate-to-distribute" model, which further pushed down interest rates of subprime mortgages, (iii) reduced underwriting criterion for the origination of subprime mortgages, and (iv) the irrational expectations set forth by consumers, who erroneously believed that housing prices would continue to rise indefinitely. Although there is some disagreement in regards to which of these factors was more influential, combined they created an unsustainable increase in home sales and a credit expansion that one day had to collapse.

The content of this book presents and in-depth analysis of several of the leading causes of the subprime crisis, as well as the subsequent measures that were used to contain a widespread economic recession. It is the aim of this book to provide the adequate information and tools for readers to gain insight on how we can prevent the same mistakes from happening again.

We begin our analysis by focusing on the underlying causes of the subprime mortgage crisis, and the extent that each economic factor had on the overall development of the greater economic collapse. We delineate the domino effect that was induced by a subprime mortgage credit expansion, and then outline how the repackaging of risky loans through MBS kept a crumbling mortgage market relatively unperceived. We present statistics pertaining to foreclosure rates, and assess the effect that these had on different sectors of the economy.

We seek to find an explanation for the expansion in subprime credit and housing prices in the early 2000s that led to the creation of a bubble. The bursting of that bubble is an essential event that unleashed an unprecedented increase in mortgage defaults. This analysis also explores an interesting question when considering public policy: Was the economic disaster that ensued caused by overzealous consumers who borrowed more than they could afford, or was it caused by institutional entities that gambled away the American economy? The insights that we uncover help us get a better overall picture of how the subprime mortgage crisis squarely placed the risk in the sector of the American economy that was least prepared to bear it, the low income, subprime borrowers.

This analysis leads us to explore another essential component in the development of the Great Recession, which was the decrease in household consumption and consumer confidence. We analyze how consumption (Marginal Propensity to Consume, MPC) reacts to wealth shocks. We analyze three channels in which MPC was affected: the direct wealth effect, the indirect effect related to feedback from non-tradeable jobs, and the effect of household leverage. We find a distinction between the way wealthier households adjusted their household consumption as opposed to poorer households; a distinction which is important when considering the broader economic implications of a reduction in household consumption.

We also analyze the effect that legal frameworks have on the expediency of the foreclosure process, as well as the execution of such. Differences in legal policy regarding foreclosures exist not only between different states, but also between different regions within those state lines. It is obvious that increasing foreclosures played a crucial role in the development of the crisis; with this investigation, we aim to gain certain insight on the impact that legal policy had on the economic destruction that occurred in specific areas.

Once an understanding of the foreclosure process is established, we begin a thorough analysis of the causes and implications of the increase in foreclosure rates. We begin this analysis by isolating the sources of initial home price decline, and how this, in turn, caused a surge in foreclosures. Further exploration into the topic includes an investigation on how foreclosed homes affected the prices of surrounding homes, and how a domino effect of economic events led to a vicious cycle of plummeting housing prices.

We explore the externalities that foreclosed homes pose on a community, and our analysis takes a close look at how these externalities metastasized to different sectors of the economy, in a manner we describe as "the contagion effect." An important aspect of our investigation deals with separating the different causes of the subprime mortgage crisis, acknowledging the magnitude of each one, and creating a narrative regarding of the importance of each one, respectively.

We transition our analysis to shed light on the post-foreclosure experiences of consumers, and how the economic environment of the period negatively affected consumer behavior. An important aspect of this analysis involves consumers' access to credit after experiencing a foreclosure. Foreclosures put a significant dent on individuals' access to credit, which in turn forces people to modify all aspects of their consumption. Examples range from the way they behave in the housing market (homeownership vs. renting) to the way they consume durable and non-durable goods.

This leads us to a section of the book that deals, mainly, with the role government played in reacting to the subprime mortgage crisis, and the tools they used to contain the destruction that began in the housing market. We explore the macroeconomic policy used by the Federal Reserve, such as the MBS buyback program, as well as other legislation enacted by different bodies of the American government with the end goal of easing the catastrophic destruction left behind by the subprime mortgage crisis. We also analyze public policy used to put the American economy on a road to recovery. Examples of such policies deal with creating greater access to affordable housing in the period after the crisis, as well as addressing the decline in credit markets.

We conclude our analysis by revisiting some of the important faults in the system that created an environment so susceptible to economic disaster. We aim to use the events that unfolded during the subprime mortgage crisis as a case study from which we can extract some insight on how we can prevent similar economic disasters from occurring.

# About the Editor

Jaime Luque joined the University of Wisconsin-Madison as Assistant Professor in the Department of Real Estate and Urban Land Economics at the Wisconsin School of Business (WSB) in September 2012. Prior to joining WSB, he was a Visiting Professor at the Carlos III University of Madrid.

Jaime's main academic research applies general equilibrium theory to mortgages and securities markets. He has also written on the economics of the European Union, including the necessity of a fiscal union and the impact of the sovereign crisis on credit markets. His recent work focuses on the role of the credit scoring technology in the evolution of the subprime mortgage market. Jaime's research has been published in journals such as *Journal of Economic Theory*, *Journal of Public Economics*, and *Regional Science and Urban Economics*. He has also written opinion pieces for the *Financial Times*, *Expansion*, *La Repubblica*, and the *Huffington Post*, as well as for the *Vox.eu*, *Eurointelligence* and *The Conversation* economics op-ed sites.

Jaime's teaching specializations at the WSB include real estate finance and urban economics.

# Contents

# Part I
# Overview of the Subprime Mortgage Crisis

# Chapter 1

# Understanding the Subprime Crisis

*In collaboration with* Thomas Sullivan
and Jeremy Scheer

It is often said that, "hindsight is 20/20", a saying which rings especially true when considering an event such as the Subprime Crisis. How could it be that economists, Wall Street executives, financial analysts, and even Ben Bernanke, the chairman of the Federal Reserve at the time, didn't see an event of this magnitude coming? In this chapter, we investigate economic indicators leading up to the subprime crisis, and we try to uncover if warning signs existed that would point to the imminent fall of the housing market. Answering these questions is crucial in shaping our understanding of how markets work, which in turn will enable us to identify warning signs to prevent events like this from happening again.

A repeated common argument during the Great Recession was that, if provided with perfect foresight on home price depreciation, economists could have predicted a substantial increase in the foreclosure rates that actually occurred. However, economists did not possess this foresight and believed the likelihood of a countrywide meltdown was highly unlikely, and therefore were unable to predict the consequences that home price depreciation had on foreclosures.

The notion that one factor could have such a profound destructive impact on an entire economy may appear astounding on the surface. When considering the U.S. economy, one that is led by exceptionally knowledgeable individuals with superior technology and research techniques, this viewpoint becomes even more unclear. What were the *ex-ante* projections of economists prior to the collapse? Could one deteriorating factor destroy an entire economy?

This chapter focuses on the destructive effect that the decline in home prices initiated as well as factors that must be taken into account for accurate analysis. The periods under consideration were before the crisis when home prices were skyrocketing, the peak of the market in mid-2006, and the decline thereafter. Our discussion is based on the seminal work by Gerardi *et al.* (2010), who attempted to determine to what magnitude investors could have foreseen the escalation of foreclosure rates and the degree that various factors played in this determination. This is an arduous task due to the fact that there are so many elements to take into consideration when examining the period leading up to the subprime crisis, as well as the crisis itself. They attempted to assert their opinion that borrowers were the most sensitive to home price depreciation, and that this price decline was the factor that actually led to the collapse of the economy. They recognized factors such as underwriting standards, leverage, documentation in lending, risk layering, and a variety of other aspects in formulating their argument, although they depicted these factors as marginal in comparison to the decline of house prices. Gerardi *et al.* collectively achieved their goal by using two samples; Massachusetts data starting in the late 1980's to capture a time of extreme house price declines prior to the Great Recession and a nationwide sample that inspects the state of the economy in the years leading up to the Great Recession. By using contrasting samples and time periods of when these models transpired, they were able to clearly identify what they believed to be the leading cause of the proliferation of defaults (decline in house prices). With this knowledge, they could assess if it was possible for economists to prevent this catastrophe beforehand.

The information regarding mortgages sold into private label market backed securities comes from the TrueStandings Securities ABS data, which is provided by First American Loan Performance. This national data is commonly used in the industry to follow the performance of mortgages in mortgage-backed securities (MBS), and it would have been used before and during the subprime crisis. Furthermore, Gerardi *et al.* (2010) restricted this data set specifically to the three most popular types of loans at the time: fixed interest rates to maturity and two types of loans at adjust called the 2/28s and 3/27s. To add to this data set, they also used data from the Standard & Poor's Case Shiller Home Price Index, state-level house price data from the Office of Federal Housing Enterprise Oversight (OFHEO), state-level unemployment rates, monthly oil prices, and interest rates. Additionally, they used data from the Census Bureau on ZIP code level data on average household income, share of minority households, share of households with a high school education or less, and the child share of the population. All of this data is used in order to have a more complete picture of the situation before they modeled their results.

Gerardi *et al.* (2010) also used a significant amount of data from the state of Massachusetts. This is publicly available information, and contains individual-level data on both housing and mortgage transactions in the state of Massachusetts, from county-level registry of deeds offices. Additionally, they used information from the Warren Group, which has followed home buyers in Massachusetts since the late 1980s. This is ownership-level data, which can include more than one mortgage loan since it spans the homeowner's time at the specific property. Even though this data was not widely used by the industry, it was available information before and during the subprime crisis and contains relevant information.

Expectations for the future of home prices are one of the driving forces in the subprime crisis. If home prices continued to appreciate, things would have been fine. However, the rate at which home prices were appreciating was unsustainable in the long-term, and eventually when the downturn came, a lot of homeowners were not in a situation where they could ride out the decline without having to foreclose on their homes. The model developed in Gerardi *et al.* (2010) aggregated all of the data gathered and tried to predict what analysts would have been able to predict prior to the Great Recession. These models proved to be pretty accurate and showed that analysts could have seen this decline in home prices coming; they just thought it was improbable.

In order to see what the financial community was thinking at the time, a combination of different parts of reports written by analysts at the five major banks, J. P. Morgan, Citigroup, Morgan Stanley, UBS, and Lehman Brothers was used. From these reports, there were some underlying themes that provided insight on the crisis. One of the main points discovered was that many analysts anticipated the possibility of a crisis in a qualitative way, even discussing potentially different ways in which it could happen, but the analysts never made measurable implications. Another important take away that adds to their main point is that analysts were remarkably optimistic about home price appreciation, which directly affected their actions. In 2006, investors expected that household prices would continue to appreciate or to plateau, not to start dropping, even though some data showed the possibility of a crash. Analysts understood that a major fall in home price appreciation would lead to a dramatic increase in problems in the subprime market, but they simply thought that a 20 percent nationwide fall in prices was impossible. These analysts chose to focus on scenarios that gave the lowest default rates, which directly affected their outlook for subprime mortgage performance.

Gerardi *et al.* (2010) main point is to prove that reduced underwriting standards alone cannot explain the dramatic rise in foreclosures. Even though it was a part of it, it was not the only cause. Although newly originated subprime loans carrying less than full documentation did increase from 1999 to 2006, they were by no means the majority of the business, nor did they increase dramatically during the credit boom.

With all of their data from ABS, S&P/Case-Shiller, and Office of Housing Enterprise Oversight, Gerardi *et al.* could estimate what an analyst with perfect foresight about home prices, interest rates, oil prices, and other variables would have predicted for prepayment and foreclosures in 2005–2007. By using the data, they created a model to predict the number of foreclosures in the fourth quarter of 2007 and then compared them to the actual numbers. The model that used data from 2000 to 2004 does very well at predicting foreclosures, accounting for approximately 85 percent of cumulative foreclosures in the fourth quarter of 2007. The model that used 2005 data did not perform as well, but it still predicted 63 percent of cumulative foreclosures in the fourth quarter of 2007. There were significant differences in the performance of the model when using the data from the two sample periods, but both can predict a majority of the foreclosures that occurred. This shows that if investors been endowed with perfect foresight about actual home price changes, then they could have predicted a significant portion of the increase in foreclosure rates that occurred, although not all of it.

The decline in home prices and housing equity were the key drivers of the foreclosures. Other factors such as underwriting standards did not deteriorate enough to explain the foreclosure. To further test how underwriting affected the housing crisis, they examined the different types of amortization schedules used at the time. Non-traditional amortization schedules started to become increasingly popular among subprime loans, and highly leveraged loans increased as well, growing from pretty much 0 percent in 2001 to close to 20 percent of subprime originations by the end of 2006.

It can be deduced that the presence of home price depreciation and diminished housing equity were the foundation of the rise in foreclosures. By no means did Gerardi *et al.* disregard related factors, although they attribute the collapse mainly to the fall in home prices nationwide. In 2000, high combined loan to value (CLTV) ratio lending accounted for around 10 percent of loan originations, which rose to over 50 percent by 2006. The notion that a growing amount of subprime loans were provided to those with high loan to value (LTV) ratios does increase the probability of default, although not to the point where it should be considered a more vital factor than home price depreciation. From 2004 to 2008, loans without a second lien had an average CLTV ratio of 79.9 percent, compared to those with a second lien had an average CLTV ratio of 98.8 percent. This indicates the use of risk layering, which similarly to the amount of high LTV ratio loans given in this time, increased. Risk layering is the process of creating loans with a combination of risk factors, such as high leverage and minimal documentation. This risk layering created a situation where the lender did not have accurate knowledge on the borrower's background. Therefore, loans were provided to individuals that would otherwise be considered too risky. They explained that documentation must be taken into account due to the fact that risk layering is commonly a result of low loan documentation, and a high CLTV ratio. During this time, documentation of loans was shaky at best, therefore providing the borrower with an opportunity to exploit the lender's services. The combination of high leverage, a high LTV ratio, poor documentation and risk layering led to a false degree of certainty that these borrowers would not default on their loans. Gerardi *et al.* took factors other than home price depreciation into account when assessing the influences of such a rapid increase in the rate of foreclosures, although they regard these factors as secondary with respect to the effect they had on the crisis as a whole.

Gerardi *et al.* (2010) ultimately concluded that economists could have predicted the reactiveness of foreclosures to home price depreciation. Their analysis indicated that they were not able to predict this reactiveness due to the optimistic view that the future value of home prices would not dramatically drop. In one example, one of the five major banking institutions mentioned earlier provided an accurate representation of what would happen in the most disastrous of situations. It stated that, "forecasting delinquencies in May 2008 with a 20 percent fall in house prices (roughly what happened), would have predicted a 35 percent delinquency rate and a 4 percent cumulative loss rate. The actual numbers for the 2006-1 asset-backed securities index (ABX) were a 39 percent delinquency rate and a 4.27 percent cumulative loss rate." These numbers are comparable to what actually happened when the recession hit, ultimately proving that economists knew the potential effects of such home price depreciation, but did not take into account the likelihood of a meltdown actually occurring. Therefore, it can be concluded that analysts did not believe such extreme home price depreciation could occur, for it they did, the foreclosures that followed could have been potentially avoided.

Mian and Sufi (2014) both support and further illustrate Gerardi *et al.* (2010) viewpoints on the housing crisis. For example, Mian and Sufi acknowledged that before the recession purchasing on credit became more acceptable, consumer's debt as percentage of household income sharply increased before the crisis, and that there was a large drop in household spending once the crises started. Although all of these factors do not directly support Gerardi *et al.* conclusions, they parallel the factors that occurred before the recession, and the effects it had during it.

Another connection between Mian and Sufi (2014) and Gerardi *et al.* (2010) is that both studies touch on the increased gap between the rich and the poor that became apparent as a result of high debt and the dramatic decline in house prices. Similarly, Mian and Sufi (2014) recognized the decline in housing prices as the driving force, although they place more emphasis on the dichotomy between the rich and the poor than do Gerardi *et al.* (2010).

One potential problem in Gerardi *et al.* (2010) is that they had to close their data set on December 2007, so they only were able to track mortgages originated through December 2006. It would be helpful to see this data throughout the entire financial crisis. Observations suggest that the relationship between housing prices and foreclosures is highly sensitive to the housing cycle. When house prices are falling, highly leveraged borrowers often will have negative equity, which limits their options. This means it would be helpful if they had data that spanned both a boom and a bust in order to better understand that even as foreclosures rise in a home price bust, prepayments will also fall. Another potential problem that is not their fault, but still affects the results of the analysis is that there is not a comprehensive national system for tracking liens on a property. This is not a problem that could be fixed unless they created this system, but it should be noted nonetheless. Additionally, their data set could have had more information about the mortgages that would have helped their prediction and analysis. For example, if the data sets had information on the points and fees of the contract, the borrower's financial wealth, or past mortgage payment problems that the lenders are aware of, these could have helped produced more accurate numbers in their analysis. Finally, a potential problem is that they did not divide the data by location. They could have split the information and data geographically or by specifics region because what was occurring in the Midwest and Northeast was different from what happening in different parts of the country, such as the West Coast. California's situation was particularly notable because it accounted for around a quarter of the nation's housing value and the Great Recession affected it harshly.

Based on potential problems found in the article, future research could be done breaking down statistics by region. This would help understand the overall picture better because, as previously mentioned, what was going on in the Midwest and Northeast was different from what happening in different parts of the country. California's situation was particularly notable because it accounted for around a quarter of the nation's housing value and the Great Recession affected it harshly. Additionally, more of the information that the lenders were aware of could be used in the analysis of mortgages. If it is available, then it could be used for future research. The points and fees of the contract, the borrower's financial wealth, or past mortgage payment problems that the lenders were aware of at the time are all relevant information that would be interesting to look into.

## Multiple Choice Questions

1. According to Gerardi *et al.* (2010), what was one of the themes presented from reports from the five major banks?

    (a) The banks wanted to completely stop lending to borrowers with little documentation

(b) **Analysts anticipated the possibility of a crisis in a qualitative way, but they never made measurable implications because they thought it was extremely improbable**

(c) The Great Recession could not have been predicted at all

(d) None of the above

**Explanation:** The correct answer is (b): Analysts before the Great Recession expected that household prices would continue to appreciate or to level out in the next couple of years. Some data that was available at the time showed the possibility of a crash, and the analysts even understood that a major fall in home price appreciation would lead to a dramatic increase in problems in the subprime market, but they simply thought that a 20 percent nationwide fall in prices was impossible. So, instead of focusing on those meltdown possibilities which ultimately happened, the analysts focused on the situations in the future that had low default rates, which directly affected their outlook for subprime mortgage performance. Banks were continuing to lend to borrowers with little documentation at the time, and according to Gerardi *et al.* (2010) the Great Recession could have been predicted.

2. According to Gerardi *et al.* (2010), which of the following is not a factor that contributed to the amount of subprime loans granted prior to the collapse of the market?

   (a) Risk Layering
   (b) Documentation status
   **(c) Home price depreciation**
   (d) Fair Isaac Corporation (FICO) scores

**Explanation:** The correct answer is (c): Risk layering resulted in borrowers receiving more loans due to uncertainty with regard to their default probability, and therefore is a factor that contributed to the amount of subprime loans granted prior to the crisis. Low documentation allowed for borrowers to receive more loans by hiding previous advances in credit that has not yet been paid back. FICO scores acted as an indicator of the probability a borrower could eventually pay back a loan. This was a vital determinant at the time considering the amount of risk layering. Home price depreciation was not taken into account until after the peak of the crisis. If house price depreciation that was going to occur was considered, it is possible for the crisis to have been avoided. The main point of Gerardi *et al.* (2010) was that if the house price declines was anticipated, economists could have taken measures to prevent some of the destruction that actually occurred.

3. According to Gerardi *et al.* (2010), which of the following affected the number of foreclosures during the Great Recession the most?

   **(a) Assumptions about home price appreciation and ultimately the large decrease in home equity values**
   (b) The growing amount of subprime loans in the market
   (c) Risk Layering
   (d) None of the above

**Explanation:** The correct answer is (a): Home price depreciation and the diminished housing equity within the market were the main cause of foreclosures during the Great Recession. Analysts thought home price appreciation would continue or even out, but it began to drop, which caused a lot of problems, especially for highly leveraged households. Even though the growing amount of subprime loans were provided to those with high LTV ratios, which increased the probability of default, and the use of risk layering, which created a situation where the lender did not have accurate knowledge on the borrower's background, were contributing factors to foreclosure during the Great Recession because loans were provided to individuals that came with risks. Gerardi *et al.* (2010) explain that home price depreciation was the most significant cause and analysts' expectations about it right before the crisis were incorrect.

## References

Gerardi, K., A. Lehnert, S. Sherlund and P. Willen (2010), "Making Sense of the Subprime Crisis", *Brookings Papers on Economic Activity* 39, 69–159.
Mian, A. and A. Sufi (2014), *House of Debt*, USA: The University of Chicago Press.

# Chapter 2

# What Caused
# the Subprime Crisis?

*In collaboration with* Connor Kepchar
and Jonah Aelyon

After recently recovering from one of the most substantial economic downturns in history, Americans are still searching for
answers as to why this downturn occurred, and how it get so bad
so quickly. There was one area of the economy that everyone
seemed to tune into in particular — the mortgage market.
Demyanyk and Van Hermert (2011) argue that the rise and fall of
the subprime mortgage market faced a boom and bust scenario in
which unsustainable growth led to a collapse of the market as a
whole.

Demyanyk and Van Hermert's (2011) analysis builds on several sections of economic data. The first section introduces how
the mortgage crisis was caused and basic data that show the
declining performance of mortgage loans through the economic
downturn. Section two presents statistics in their database. In section three, they use an econometric analysis to explain how the
rise in foreclosures occurred, how they affected both delinquency
as well as rapidly rising foreclosure rates. In the next section, they
discuss the importance in realizing what a significant effect that
high loan-to-value (LTV) borrowers had on the housing bubble

bursting, and also work to point out the awareness level of the securitizing parties. In the fifth section, they analyze how interest rates on subprime mortgages are higher than on prime mortgages, and how the rate spread between these affected the mortgage crisis. The sixth section proves the strength in their arguments by adding variables to their original analysis. Finally, the conclusion works to bring all of their research together by thoroughly proving the thesis.

The data used in Demyanyk and Van Hermert's (2011) first work present statistics pertaining to subprime mortgage loans issued between 2001 and 2006, and how this market grew dramatically over this period. They then go on to show the results of the regression that they put together to analyze loans that were delinquent or in foreclosure within the first 12 months of origination. By analyzing the descriptive characteristics of these loans, one is able to paint a clearer picture of what caused subprime mortgages to soar in the early 2000s.

Demyanyk and Van Hermert (2011) utilized a logit regression model in order to explain the high level of mortgage delinquencies and foreclosures in vintage 2006 mortgage loans. The event in the regression is either a delinquency or foreclosure with a loan after a given number of months. This event is the dependent variable in the regression. A delinquency is defined as payments being 60 or more days late, and foreclosure as defined as a property being owned by a lender. However, after a loan is finalized, or the balance is zero, the loan is not counted in the analysis. In looking at borrower and loan characteristics within the regression, they examine the Fair Isaac Corporation (FICO) credit score, the combined loan-to-debt ratio, the debt-to-income ratio, and several other dummy variables. These dummy variables include one indicating whether the loan was cash-out refinancing, whether the debt-to-income ratio was present, whether the borrower was an investor or an owner–occupier, whether full documentation was provided to receive the loan, whether there is a prepayment penalty on the loan, the mortgage rate, and the margin for adjustable rate and hybrid loans. The final variable measures how a home has appreciated from the time of loan origination to when the property is evaluated as delinquent or in foreclosure. Together, these variables work to prove through econometric analysis that loan quality deteriorated monotonically between 2001 and 2006.

The results of Demyanyk and Van Hermert's (2011) model tests and sensitivity analyses conducted allows one to observe that yes, loan quality did in fact decrease between 2001 and 2006 as previously stated. It is important to note that the quality of the loans did not decrease equally amongst the different borrows. High-LTV borrowers were clearly a riskier investment from the lender's point of view, rightfully. When comparing high-LTV borrowers with low-LTV one's, an extremely strong correlation can be observed between the mortgage rate and the LTV ratio. Essentially pioneered by Wells Fargo, the most important measure of debt is the debt yield, which looks at net operating income's (NOI) percentage of the total loan amount. Commercial real-estate lenders believe that this is the most indicative metric of a borrower's ability to repay a loan. Although there are many other financial metrics to consider, at the end of a day a lender is only concerned with the borrower's ability to repay the loan and a higher-LTV suggests less skin in the game, thus making it easier to walk out on the loan, resulting in a foreclosure. In 2001, when a borrower LTV was just one-standard deviation above average, they paid a 10 basis point premium. By 2006, this premium climbed up to 30 basis points. The subprime–prime mortgage spread acted counter-intuitively. One would assume that the mark-up would decline over time, when in fact it did the complete opposite which in turn favored the riskier loans. The subprime mortgage market crashed in 2007 as history shows and it followed an apparently "classic" pattern. Institutional investors saw the free-money opportunity within mortgage-backed-security (MBS), which ultimately vastly increased the demand of mortgages. Lenders responded to this with an increase in supply. However, the increase in supply then manifested by the lenders, was one of deteriorated quality. The underwriting standards were weakened which resulted in worse performing loans, and risk premiums that no longer made logical sense.[1]

The mortgage market acted completely differently than it had been assumed to be performing, which all lends itself to the asset-bubble burst, heavily relating this chapter to the thoughts presented by Mian and Sufi in their book, *House of Debt*. Another important book to highlight when discussing the subprime mortgage crisis is *The Big Short* by Michael Lewis. Lewis (2010) discusses a few brilliant individuals who noticed all of the issues that Demyanyk and Van Hermert (2011) and Mian and Sufi (2014) discuss, and literally bet against the entire United States Economy. The idea that the rapid increase in housing prices nationally gave room for a perceived substantial increase in value shows that nobody besides the individuals highlighted by Lewis really understood what our economy was doing. When house prices stopped climbing, it was quite apparent that the level of risk had grown substantially. The core of Lewis' argument discusses the increase in demand for these MBS, which in turn led to bankers not performing their fiduciary responsibilities to the entire US Economy. The Levered-Losses framework, a model created by Mian and Sufi (2014) also gets at the root of the financial crisis. The fact that a collapse in asset prices when an economy has such elevated debt levels, can only lead to a massive economic disaster. This is exactly what happened following the subprime mortgage crisis. What Mian and Sufi (2014) do discuss however, is that the recession is preceded by a sharp run-up in household debt which is not the point that Demyanyk and Van Hermert (2011) discuss nor is it one Lewis (2010) highlights. Demyanyk and Van Hermert suggest that the run-up in household debt was due to the increased ease of getting a mortgage because of the loosened lending standards, which was all fueled by the institutional US and foreign investors sinking their capital into MBS, money-making machines.

---

[1] See Luque and Riddiough (2016) for a theoretical model of the role of the credit scoring technology in the rise and subsequent dominance of the subprime conduit mortgage market.

A major weakness present in Demyanyk and Van Hermert's (2011) argument is the poor organization. There are many times when a reader will need to find a previously shown chart or visual, as well as the organization of topics being unclear to follow. Additionally, due to the nature and length of an academic paper, it is easy to lose sight of Demyanyk and Van Hermert's goal and what questions they are trying to answer. They could do a better job of reminding the audience every so often the main goal or question of the research paper, and how it has since then given data to support an ultimate conclusion. When reading the end of the argument, it is difficult to grasp one concrete conclusion and answer to the question at hand. The introduction and conclusion should be able to both be read and give someone a great working knowledge, without the list of data, of the subject at hand.

One recommendation for future research is to take a closer look at the actual MBS securitized deals. When actually analyzing a structured finance deal one is able to get a better insight into the actual loans themselves and what is going on behind the scenes — the secondary market. Unless an average-citizen is explained the subprime mortgage crisis thoroughly, they are unaware of the big institutional MBS players and how they effected the crisis. It simply appears to be that the lenders weakened their standards; people could not pay their loans, therefore, financial meltdown. It is a lot more complex than that.

## Multiple Choice Questions

1. According to Demyanyk and Van Hemert (2011), what is the most important macroeconomic factor that the subprime mortgage crisis can be attributed to?

   **(a) House Price Appreciation**
   (b) House Price Depreciation
   (c) Interest rate decline
   (d) Interest rate increase

**Explanation:** The correct answer is (a): Demyanyk and Van Hemert (2011) look at the difference in home value between the time of the loan's origination and the time of the loan's performance valuation (within the first 1.5 years), and find that it was very common .... during this time period for people to witness an appreciation in their home price, and to then take out a home equity line of credit. This is a way of using a home as an asset to take an additional loan from the bank with extremely favorable terms. While the investors continued to buy the mortgages through the secondary market, everyone believed the prices were skyrocketing, but at the first sign of a decrease in home value, the risk in the market was easily visible.

2. According to Demyanyk and Van Hermert (2011), in which years between 2001 and 2007 did we see the worst performance of the loans?

   (a) 2001–2002
   (b) 2002–2003
   (c) 2003–2004
   (d) 2004–2005
   (e) 2005–2006
   **(f) 2006–2007**

**Explanation:** The years in which the most inferior performance occurred in the loans was 2006 and 2007. The loans originated in these years had the highest delinquency rates. These constitutes as not paying any loan payments for 60 days. These loans "benefited" from a substantially weakened lending environments, which meant the standards had weakened greatly. The years to come now will be quite interesting in the MBS markets as many of the awful loans created during 2006 and 2007 are about to mature since they hold 10 year terms. There is about to be a big shake up in MBS.

3. What two rates did Demyanyk and Van Hermert (2011) focus on throughout their study to prove the cause of the subprime mortgage crisis?

   (a) Foreclosure and LTV
   (b) Delinquency and Appreciation
   (c) Appreciation and Depreciation
   **(d) Foreclosure and Delinquency**

**Explanation:** Foreclosure and Delinquency rates are the two focuses of the research that Demyanyk and Van Hermert (2011) conducted. They found that while other loan description characteristics may not tell the whole story, and may not be fully correlated to when the mortgage crisis was at its worst, the foreclosure and delinquency rates always correlated to the ups and downs of the subprime mortgage crisis. In order to get the best understanding of how the subprime mortgage collapse occurred, one must pay attention to when property loans started having trouble in terms of being paid off, and being taken over completely in foreclosure.

## References

Demyanyk, Y. and O. Van Hermert (2011), "Understanding the Subprime Mortgage Crisis", *The Review of Financial Studies*, 24, 1848–1880.
Lewis, M. (2010), *The Big Short: Inside the Doomsday Machine*, W. W. Norton.
Mian, A. and A. Sufi (2014), *House of Debt*, USA: The University of Chicago Press.

# Chapter 3
# Mortgage Credit Expansion

*In collaboration with* Eric Duwe and Hyung Jin Kim

In order to get an adequate understanding of the events that led up to the subprime mortgage crisis, it is pertinent to first analyze the period of major credit expansion and increased homeownership that occurred between 2000 and 2006. What economic factors created incentives for this extraordinary increase in credit and home sales? Was this caused by a positive consumer wealth effect arising from the reduced cost of borrowing? Could an irresponsible expansion in risky lending be to blamed? Or were consumers guided by an irrational expectation of rising house prices? Pinpointing the source of this expansion can aid us in comprehending consumer behavior.

Mian and Sufi (2009) attempt to tackle one of the central questions behind the most damaging economic downturn in the United States since the 1930s — why did subprime lending and housing prices expand so rapidly in the early 2000s, creating a bubble that burst and unleashed a mortgage default crisis unprecedented in modern American history?

Using micro-level data and empirical analysis, Mian and Sufi (2009) examine three competing hypotheses advanced by various experts and economists. The first is an *income-based hypothesis* arguing that subprime borrowers, for whatever reason, experienced a rise in disposable income over the period of increased lending, allowing them to take out potentially riskier mortgages when buying new homes. The second is a *supply-based hypothesis*, arguing that, for various reasons, the supply of mortgages expanded during this period of time, allowing for an increased amount of lending to borrowers who may not have been able to secure loans in the past. The third explanation is an *expectations-based hypothesis*, asserting that lenders did not anticipate a slow in the rapid growth of home prices, or did not perceive the existence of a housing bubble at all, leading to an increased willingness to lend to potentially unreliable borrowers.

In analyzing consumer debt and credit scores, Mian and Sufi (2009) utilized data from the Analytical Services group at Equifax, which included distributions of outstanding credit with corresponding credit scores. The total final sample of 18,408 ZIP codes, which represented 92 percent of entirety of U.S., corresponded to the ZIP code level data on mortgage loans from the Home Mortgage Disclosure Act (HDMA) from 1990 to 2007 minus ZIP codes without Equifax or HDMA data. House price data produced from Fiserv's Case Shiller Weiss (FCSW) indices, representing years 1990–2008, took advantage of repeated sales data of a same-house resulting in a ZIP-level price index. FCSW data is limited, provided that it only contains price data of a mere 3,014 ZIP codes from the Equifax-HMDA sample, totaling 16 percent of all ZIP codes. However, this data nonetheless represent more than 45 percent of aggregate outstanding consumer debt. Additional Census data include demographics such as population, poverty, education, unemployment, wages, business establishments, etc. from 1996 to 2004. On top of Census data, some IRS gross income data also contributes to Mian and Sufi's (2009) hypothesis. Finally, the *CAP Index* provides ZIP-level total crime statistics from 2000 through 2007.

Using data on subprime lending and incomes from comparisons between both Metropolitan Statistical Areas (MSA) and ZIP codes, Mian and Sufi (2009) present an analysis that points to flaws in the income-based approach to the subprime question. When comparing data between MSAs in the United States from 2002 to 2005, it appears that MSAs with higher proportions of subprime borrowers (those with credit scores <660), like the Houston Metropolitan Area, experienced levels of income growth higher than their counterparts with lower numbers of subprime borrowers. These MSAs also experienced higher levels of credit growth overall.

However, when Mian and Sufi (2009) examined similar data at the smaller ZIP code level, they saw different results. At this micro-level of analysis, ZIP codes with higher proportions of subprime borrowers actually experienced negative income growth between 2002 and 2005. At the same time, these ZIP codes experienced higher levels of credit growth overall, leading to the conclusion that there exists a possible negative correlation between credit expansion and income growth during the time period in question, a correlation that was not observed in previous historical periods of credit expansion that Mian and Sufi examined. They therefore dismiss the income-based hypothesis and move on to examine the supply-based hypothesis.

Mian and Sufi (2009) found data to show that the expansion in the mortgage supply leading to the subprime lending boom was stronger than the data for the income-based hypothesis. Rates of denial for subprime lenders fell dramatically at the beginning of the credit and housing price boom in 2002. This suggests an increased willingness on the part of lenders to approve riskier loans. There also was a significant increase in the securitization of subprime mortgages during this time, where banks packaged high-risk mortgages together and sold them off as assets to third parties — the number of securitized mortgages quickly skyrocketed from 30 percent to 60 percent. This increase occurred disproportionately within subprime borrower-dominated ZIP codes, and these ZIP codes experienced some of the highest rates of default beginning in 2005, all suggesting that mortgage lenders may have engaged in reckless or hazardous lending in the years prior to the crisis.

The *income-based hypothesis* expresses a negative correlation, unlike during any other time period than 2002–2005. The hypothesis does not justify the changing environment in the business as the reason for increase in income of subprime households; in the past 18 years, income growth and mortgage expansion demonstrated negative correlation only during the subprime crisis. The distinct negative correlation between income and mortgage credit implies variations of mortgage credit supply, which the *supply-based hypothesis* also upholds.

The *supply-based hypothesis* relies on a decrease in the subprime-prime interest rate between 2002 and 2005. A fall in interest rates took place while the supply and risks of subprime mortgages increased, producing Mian and Sufi's ZIP-level analysis to show results consistent to the *supply-based hypothesis*. Other factors contributing to the *supply-based hypothesis* include: increased denial of credit that preceded subprime mortgage expansion; the negative correlation between mortgage and income growth with subprime mortgage expansion; sharper increases in mortgage securitization in subprime ZIP codes compared to prime ZIP codes; and a dramatic increase in default rates beginning in 2005.

According to Mian and Sufi (2009), their ZIP code level house price index displays an inordinate increase in house prices for subprime ZIP codes during the crisis. In order to explain the relationship between house price growth and subprime mortgage expansion, Mian and Sufi questioned the validity of house prices in their *expectations-based* hypothesis, where expansion in mortgage credit from 2002 to 2005, as well as increase in house price resulted from lenders' high house price expectations and expansion in credit supply. However, price expectations alone do not justify the hypothesis, because mortgage credit expansion should not have been prevalent in areas with elastic housing supply such as Wichita, Kansas, where house prices depend on construction costs. Consequently, the *expectations-based hypothesis* does not suffice as an explanation for mortgage credit growth.

The combination of results from Mian and Sufi's (2009) hypothesis, with 2002–2005 being the only period that displays negative correlation between income growth and mortgage credit expansion, suggest possibilities of increased house prices due to raised credit supply. However, Mian and Sufi (2009) state that an accurate interpretation may require more evidence through further research.

Mian and Sufi (2009) highlight that the evidence showed increases in defaults resulting in growth in mortgage credit. Low risk-free rates from 2001 through 2005 likely sparked the beginning of the subprime mortgage credit expansion. Elasticity of housing supply and other local housing elements also deliver effects leading towards credit growth. Complementary indications include fall in denial rates, decrease in subprime–prime interest spreads, and increase in subprime mortgage securitization.

Much of the mortgage growth mentioned by Mian and Sufi (2009) appears in Mian and Sufi's (2014) book, *House of Debt*. There is a close relationship with Mian and Sufi's (2014) which pertains to explaining how the mortgage crisis brought multiple consequences and eventually led to the most severe economic crisis; "the mortgage default rate for the entire country had never risen above 6.5 percent. By 2009 it spiked above 10 percent." Evidence shown in Mian and Sufi (2014) resembles, or in some cases originates from, those provided in Mian and Sufi (2009). For example, hypothesis based on Fair Isaac Corporation (FICO) scores and default probabilities appear in both studies. In fact, the main points argued in Mian and Sufi (2014) are in favor of all hypotheses and suggestions provided in Mian and Sufi (2009).

Conclusively, Mian and Sufi (2009) lean towards the *supply-based hypothesis* compared to *income-based* and *expectations-based*. However, methods of direct influence towards credit supply are absent, and therefore more evidence is required in order to produce an accurate claim. Control over a large sample and the identification of variables challenge any research; economic assumptions cannot avoid these uncertainties. Therefore, in order to develop an accurate argument, careful collection of data over time along with more examples from domestic and foreign financial crisis may facilitate later research.

Ultimately, the chapter provides details about the mortgage expansion crisis by illustrating possible driving forces behind the scenes. Although some factors limit the authors' ability to develop an accurate argument with causality, they successfully portray various elements that come into play before, during, and after the crisis. However, this illustration of the crisis using data, statistics, and economic intuition may not suffice to explain the entirety of the phenomenon. For instance, borrowers and lenders who are understood to be rational actors exhibited unique behavior that does not completely explain the motives for certain actions. The continuation of similar studies, however, will most likely dissect the worst economic crisis of U.S. history, providing methods to avoid such disasters.

## Multiple Choice Questions

1. According to Mian and Sufi (2009), what was the correlation between income growth and mortgage credit expansion from 2002 to 2005, and how does it differ to other time periods?

   (a) There was no correlation; normally income and mortgage growth has positive correlation

   (b) There was no correlation; normally income and mortgage growth has negative correlation

   **(c) There was a negative correlation; normally income and mortgage growth has positive correlation**

   (d) There was a positive correlation; normally income and mortgage growth has negative correlation

**Explanation:** The answer is (c): In fact, 2002 through 2005 was the only period in which income growth and mortgage credit growth had negative correlation. Normally, the correlation is positive. Mian and Sufi explain that the shift in credit supply most likely causes the negative correlation, while direct causality assumption is impossible due to lack of control over data.

2. According to Mian and Sufi (2009), which of the following regarding the mortgage default crisis is true?

   (a) Consumers with credit scores below 660 had acceptable credit reputation

   (b) Consumers with credit scores below 660 had lower default probability

   **(c) Consumers with credit scores below 660 were represented by 29 percent of consumers in a ZIP code as of 1996**

    (d) Consumers with credit scores below 660 were represented by 29 percent of consumers in a ZIP code as of 2002

**Explanation:** The answer is (c): On average, 29 percent of consumers in a ZIP code had lower credit scores than 660 as of 1996. On the other hand, borrowers with FICO scores above 660 were deemed to have acceptable credit reputations. These borrowers displayed much lower probability of default.

3. According to Mian and Sufi (2009), which of the following statements is true about causality behind the mortgage expansion crisis?

    (a) Income growth leads to more borrowing. Therefore, income growth is the definite cause of mortgage expansion

    (b) Expectations of high house prices lead to more borrowing, and results in mortgage expansion

    (c) Decrease in income leads to more borrowing. Therefore, income growth is the definite cause of mortgage expansion

    **(d) Lenders increasing supply of credit could be one of the driving factors that lead to mortgage expansion**

    (e) Mortgage credit expansion originates from an increase in credit supply caused by high risk-free rates

**Explanation:** Mian and Sufi emphasize that direct causality assumption is not possible due to limitations on instruments of controlling credit supply. However, after careful analysis of *income-based*, *expectations-based*, and *supply-based hypothesis*, Mian and Sufi conclude that the rise of subprime mortgages shows a strong correlation with credit supply, driven by factors such as low risk-free rates, lowered denial rates and other patterns.

## References

Mian, A. and A. Sufi (2009), "The Consequences of Mortgage Credit Expansion: Evidence from the U.S. Mortgage Default Crisis", *Quarterly Journal of Economics* 124, 1449–1496.

Mian, A. and A. Sufi (2014), *House of Debt*, USA: The University of Chicago Press.

# Chapter 4
# Household Consumption

*In collaboration with* Harold Young and Carl Miller

Households make consumption decisions by maximizing their level of utility subject to their budget constraint. When negative wealth shocks affect a household's budget, consumption decisions must be adjusted accordingly. The fall in property values that followed the bursting of the housing bubble is an example of such a shock, and it effectively had an impact on consumers' behavior. A decrease in consumption sends ripples through the economy, and can exacerbate an already negative economic climate. Understanding how consumption was affected by the subprime crisis is crucial in ascertaining how a crisis in a specific sector affects the economy as a whole.

Living in the area code of 626 in southern California, one realizes that Pasadena would be an excellent place to live. The Rose Bowl is very close, the school systems are great, and the crime rates are relatively low. Taking into account these reasons, it is very expensive to live in that area. As is the case with most cities, some houses are more expensive than others, but from the data collected from the first two months of years 2006–2009 it can be understood how the economy within this particular city was affected. The data found from The Pasadena-Foothills Association of REALTORS encompasses 361 homes in the 626 area code. The average housing price was $740,663.24. This number helps one understand the types of homes in the area; however, imagine if the homes sold in this area were all large value houses that skew the data. This is not so, due the average price per square foot (price/sqft) of all these houses and the percent change in said price used to buttress this information. The height of the market within the data set was 2008, when the average housing price was $872,682.07 and the price/sqft was $465.75. In 2009, the crash hit and caused the price/sqft to fall to $351.20. This is a 24.59 percent change in the price, which is an average loss of $214,628.44, per house. The data prove that no matter what neighborhood one lives in, the market has affected everyone including those that are considered "high value" neighborhoods. Now, we compare this example to the work in Mian, Rao, and Sufi (2013).

Mian, Rao, and Sufi (2013) aim to describe the housing collapse of 2006–2009. In particular, they attempt to discover how consumption reacts to large negative shocks to household net worth, and if households with differing wealth levels have differing Marginal Propensities to Consume (MPC). MPC in the context of housing wealth shows the dollar value decline in an individual's spending in response to wealth shocks.

To begin their research Mian, Rao, and Sufi (2013) identify three channels in which the average estimated MPC was affected: the direct wealth effect, indirect effect related to feedback from non-tradable jobs, and household leverage. Non-tradeable jobs are those which provide goods and services for local economies such as barbers, retail stores, etc. They draw from Carroll and Kimball's (1996) findings that state the consumption of low-net worth households react more radically to changes in income in comparison to high-net worth households. Mian, Rao, and Sufi (2013) found that there was a strong relationship between the change in home value and the change in their spending. According to the data the authors found, net worth declined on average $48,000 with some losses exceeding $150,000. They also found average household spending decreased on average $1,700. They noticed a trend in their data in which households with the greatest leverage experienced the greatest losses. Based off of this theory the authors were able to estimate that the average MPC was 5.4 cents/$. To further their point, the ZIP codes hit the hardest with the housing shock experiencing a MPC of 9.4 cents/$. In summary, their findings indicate a larger decline in housing net worth that was caused by a decrease in home price and homeowners leverage levels.

In Mian, Rao, and Sufi (2013) theory of levered households, they focus on the terms elastic and inelastic housing supply. Elastic housing supply is defined as cities in which there are no geographic barriers to expansion. This means that as the city grows in population it can develop more land (build new infrastructure, housing, etc.). In contrast, inelastic housing supply is a city which is spatially constrained, usually by physical barriers (mountains, bodies of water, etc.), in which the city cannot ease space constraints by developing more. They use housing supply elasticity to compare and contrast home value and the effects of the shock on each. What they found was cities with an inelastic housing supply, generally speaking, are much more levered and experienced a much higher run-up in home prices in the years leading up to the shock. During this run, homeowners in these areas levered up against the rising value of their homes. When the shock occurred home values in these areas plummeted as seen in the example of Pasadena. The authors discovered the households with the greatest leverage experienced the greatest decline in net worth. Homeowners in areas that experienced the largest net-worth shocks saw on average decreases in household net worth of 26 percent. The rapid loss in net worth of homeowners combined with the high leverage caused many in these highly levered areas to default on their debts. At the height of the shock in 2009 roughly 5 percent of mortgages nationally were in foreclosure. Meanwhile, households with the least amount of leverage, about 20 percent or lower loan-to-value ratio (LTV), experienced very little net worth effects and were mainly unaffected by the shock due to diversification of their assets. The least levered households were far more likely to have a large savings as well as investments in stocks and bonds. Housing values plummeted about 30 percent during the shock and were very slow to return to prior levels. On the contrary, stocks crashed in 2008–2009 but rebounded exceptionally in the years following, while the bond markets thrived during the shock. With this being said, those with low leverage and diversified assets lost some money, but they saw that money recovered in the years following. Meanwhile, those with high leverage in their homes lost massive amounts of money with much of that money never returning. Based off of these findings the authors were able to reject the hypothesis that the financial crisis was completely risk sharing in which all households equally shared the negative effects. It is very clear that the poorest households bear the majority of the risk.

The large net worth declines also affected households' consumption habits. While compiling their evidence, Mian, Rao, and Sufi (2013) were able to estimate that decreases in consumption were caused by a $5.6 trillion loss in home value from 2006 to 2009. They also were able to estimate a total decline in spending of about $870 billion between 2006 and 2009. These numbers suggest that richer ZIP codes have a lower spending sensitivity to the same decline in home price.

Furthering their research, Mian, Rao, and Sufi (2013) use ZIP code level auto registration information from RL Polk from the years 1998 to 2012. They looked at the counties and ZIP codes of new vehicle registrations throughout the country. They found that wealth inequality was more pronounced in ZIP codes rather than across counties. ZIP codes offered much more reliable data and truly showed the fluctuations in the wealth gap. It is estimated that out of $870 billion in losses $330 billion came from the auto sales sector alone. Based off of this evidence, the average decline in MPC for auto spending was 1.8 cents/$. Furthermore, ZIP codes in which housing leverage was below 30 percent slash auto spending by about 1 cent/$ lost. Meanwhile, households with housing leverage of 90 percent or greater experience a 3 cent decline in auto spending per dollar decline in home value. Using this information, they also found that households with an adjusted gross income (AGI) of less than $35,000 carried an MPC that was three times greater than households with an AGI greater than $200,000. In conclusion, they found that wealthier households have a much smaller MPC out of housing wealth in comparison to poor households.

Lastly, Mian, Rao, and Sufi (2013) relied on the impact of debt on the consumer and economy as a whole. They used MasterCard data to measure household consumption spending. This data was used to measure total spending in a county broken into three categories: durable goods, groceries, and other non-durable goods. The authors then analyzed household net worth to compare how the shock effected different income levels. They categorized household net worth into housing assets, financial assets, and debt. Using this information, they create a house price index and are able to estimate the change in homeownership and population growth. To test this, they use ZIP code data to determine the housing leverage (LTV). They found that the higher the LTV the higher the risk of foreclosure. The higher the housing leverage for a household combined with a lower net value amplify the effect of the housing decline on spending. They also found that a decrease in home value leads to tighter credit constraints, reduced home equity, reduced credit card limits, declines in refinancing volume, and increases in subprime borrowing within the ZIP code. This again focuses the losses on the poorest households. It was these poorest households who needed to take advantage of ultra-low-interest rates the most; however, due to their deteriorated credit and low savings they were not able to do so. Those with an LTV of 36 percent or below saw a decline in refinance rates of only 8 cents/$ of home value lost. Meanwhile, the 90 percent or higher group saw refinance rates of 17 cents/$ of home value lost. These data imply that credit constraints were much larger for ZIP codes with the lowest household income and that the housing leverage ratio was independent to both income and leverage. They found that lending linked to housing collateral was the main channel in which the household leverage ratio applies.

In summary, the main takeaways from this study is that the large effect of housing net worth shocks on consumption reduce spending by 5.4–7.2 cents/$ of housing wealth loss. The data implied that the impact of wealth shocks relied on the total wealth lost and how the losses were distributed across the country. Lastly, high levels of private debt and/or a significant reduction in consumption can lead to recessions.

The findings of this chapter relate with other academic writing that focuses on levered homes within an area and how the nature behind these homes affects the economy during recessions. Mian and Sufi (2014) explain how the nature of levered homes affects the economy. They describe the phenomenon in which the homeowner has taken on a large sum of debt in comparison to the home value. When the housing bubble burst the value of the home plummeted leaving the homeowner severely indebted. In the case of the most recent shock many people purchased homes with astronomical LTV ratios and when prices dropped their share of ownership in the property dropped significantly, often times to zero. They use an example in which a homeowner purchases a house worth $100,000 was financed with 80 percent debt. When the housing price dropped 20 percent the homeowner lost all of their investment. Mian and Sufi (2014) ties nicely with Mian, Rao, and Sufi (2013) and provides the reader with a further understanding of the levered loss framework and its effects on MPC.

While Mian, Rao, and Sufi (2013) make great points with the information they found from MasterCard users, they leave out information about homeowners and the change in their MPC. While it can be convenient for them to say that credit card users have the same spending preferences across all credit card companies, this information cannot be assumed. They fail to uncover data on three of the four major credit card companies. Visa, American Express, and Discover are credit card companies that are not even mentioned within the paper which leads to concerns about the accuracy of their findings in regard to users MPC. While it would be beneficial to have data from all four major credit card companies, it is understood that it's inconceivable to expect the authors to collect and analyze all that information. One can disagree with their notion that leaving the other three companies out is statistically irrelevant. Based off of this, one would suggest that future researchers should focus on different types and classes of credit cards. This additional data will either support or shed a new light on the effects of MPC across varying cardholders. For example, those with an American Express black card (Centurion card) would be a great addition to the case of MPC change during the years of 2006–2009. Including these cardholders in the data allow for one to look at the highest income brackets. The requirements of the Centurion card require the user to spend at least $250,000 a year. This will also shed light on the notion of whether or not those that have the card were as levered as those who do not. This is just one focus for future research. Another focus, albeit a large undertaking would be to get the same percentage of American Express, Visa, and Discover card holder's information to show the average MPC gain. Despite this research yielding data that is many times larger than that used for the current research by the authors, it would show an average of the national credit card population rather than a much smaller sample from only MasterCard users.

In spite of the recommendations for future research, the findings within Mian, Rao, and Sufi (2013) research are essential to discussions regarding the most recent housing shock. The findings they present the reader with, provide excellent detail and realizations that many other experts have chosen to ignore. Mian, Rao, and Sufi (2013) presentation of their findings make it convincing that arguments claiming shared losses in the shock are untrue. Furthermore, they are able to convey the importance of the levered losses framework and the role it played in concentrating losses on the poor. Overall, the work done by Mian, Rao, and Sufi (2013) is well articulated and provides the framework for thought provoking discussions.

## Multiple Choice Questions

1. According to Mian, Rao, and Sufi (2013) out of the following choices that describes the monetary net worth of households, which suffers the most from levered losses?
   (a) **The poorest net worth households**
   (b) The richest net worth households
   (c) The median net worth households
   (d) The average net worth household

**Explanation:** The correct answer is (a): The poorest suffer the most in the current structure due to several reasons. One of those reasons is that the concentration of debt and risk is focused on the borrower while the lender holds the safest position. With that being said, a borrower who puts a down payment of $20,000 for a $100,000 home holds only a 20 percent interest in the home while the lender holds an 80 percent interest. If home prices drop 20 percent, the borrowers share now drops to 0 percent equity while the lender holds a 100 percent stake. The wealthiest households typically are well diversified in other assets and they generally put a larger down payment on the home. Both of these factors protect them from default risk and lower their exposure to levered losses.

2. According to Mian, Rao, and Sufi (2013), a large effect of housing net worth shocks on consumption reduce spending by?
   (a) 15–17 cents/$1
   **(b) 5–7 cents/$1**
   (c) 1–3 cents/$1
   (d) 10–12 cents/$1

**Explanation:** The correct answer is (b): According to the data compiled by Mian, Rao, and Sufi the correct answer is between 5 and 7 cents/$. This figure is compiled from their findings that households are willing to give up roughly that amount per every dollar decrease in their homes value. As mentioned in the above question the losses are much more focused on the poorest households, but for the most part every household will decrease their consumption if their home value decreases. The 5–7 cent figure is the average amount determined in their research.

3. According to Mian, Rao, and Sufi (2013), why do levered households have higher MPCs?
   (a) Credit constraints get looser when home values decrease
   (b) Credit constraints get tighter when home values increase
   (c) Credit constraints get looser when home values increase
   **(d) Credit constraints get tighter when home values decrease**

**Explanation:** The correct answer is (d): Mian, Rao, and Sufi (2013) use four different measures to reach this conclusion. They look at the change in home equity, change in credit limit, change in refinancing volume, and finally change in percentage of the population with a credit score below 660. After examining these four factors the authors determined that the higher the leverage for the household means that credit constraints get tighter. This makes sense because as household net worth decreases as the value of the home decreases they will be stretched thinner financially which in turn will tighten their credit constraints.

## References

"The Pasadena-Foothills Association of Realtors" (2015) *The Pasadena-Foothills Association of Realtors.* N.p., n.d. Web. 17 October 2015

Mian, A. and A. Sufi (2014), *House of Debt*, USA: The University of Chicago Press.

Mian, A., K. Rao and A. Sufi (2013), "Household Balance Sheets, Consumption, and the Economic Slump", *Quarterly Journal of Economics* 128, 1687–1726.

# Chapter 5

# Judicial Requirements
# for Foreclosures

*In collaboration with* Meaghan Pauli and Luke Sidoti

As a result of the falling property values that followed the bursting of the housing bubble, many people saw their investments plummet. Some cases were so extreme that the value of homes was underwater, meaning they owed more on it than it was actually worth. Many were forced to foreclose on their homes. Foreclosing a home essentially means vacating it and turning it over to the bank after inability to service the loan. Widespread foreclosures not only have a negative impact on the values of surrounding properties, but they also negatively affect securities packaged from a bad loan. Could legal environments in communities affect the likelihood of foreclosures to happen?

"Fire sale! Everything must go!" Usually when a consumer hears those words, it is music to his or her ears. The fire sale can only mean one thing: extremely low prices. The sellers are at the point where there is a need to get the product out of their hands. Every second they hold on to their product it is depreciating in value, and they are losing money. This would be great at a garage sale, but unfortunately this is not a story about a great sale in a neighbor's garage. This is the story of the sale of a neighbor's house.

The financial crisis of 2008 was one that brought the United States to its knees. Across the United States, people were losing their homes to foreclosure as a result of, what is called today, the "subprime crisis." Foreclosures had an adverse effect on the economy, which only sent the economy into a tailspin. Depending on the state, foreclosures were handled differently. Was there a way the U.S. could have conducted these foreclosures to mitigate the economic destruction caused by them?

The goal of Mian *et al.* (2015) was, "to estimate the effect of foreclosures on economic outcomes by taking advantage of differences in state laws in the foreclosure process." Mian, Sufi, and Trebbi looked at the difference in state laws by looking at two different types of states: judicial and non-judicial. The study looked at all states and ZIP codes across the U.S. through the end of 2012. The authors looked at how the foreclosure laws affect house prices and supply, residential investment, and durable consumption. In order to see the economic effect of foreclosures, the study pulled data from many sources.

Mian *et al.* (2015) used several data sources. RealtyTrac.com provided foreclosure data at the ZIP code level from 2006 to 2013 on a yearly basis. Fiserv Case Shiller Weiss (FCSW) and Zillow.com were used for their data on house prices at the ZIP code level on a quarterly basis. Both sources were used because FCSW only went through 2010, and Zillow.com had data through 2012. CoreLogic also provided house price data through 2012. Data on new residential permits was from the U.S. Census. Auto sales data was given by R.L. Polk at the ZIP code level through 2012 on a monthly basis. The study also looked at delinquencies and credit scores by ZIP code, all of which were provided by Equifax through 2013. Lastly, the 2000 Decennial Census provided demographic information. While most sources provide data on a ZIP code level, there are some holes in each source. Each source is missing ZIP codes, especially with respect to house prices. The data are the worst in rural ZIP codes. By combining all of these sources, the information gathered covers all of the U.S.

Mian *et al.* (2015) used the difference in state laws as an instrument to compare foreclosures in similar areas. They focused on the difference in the foreclosure process between states. There are two different types of foreclosure law states: judicial and non-judicial states.

In a judicial foreclosure state, lenders must file a notice with a judge providing evidence regarding the amount of the debt, the delinquency of the debt, and why the delinquency should allow the lender to sell the property. After the filing, borrowers have an opportunity to respond. Then, the filing goes to court and if the lender is correct, the property will go to auction.

In a non-judicial foreclosure state, the original mortgage document automatically gives the lender the right to sell the property if the borrower is delinquent. The lender does not need court approval to auction a property. The lender sends a notice of default to the borrower and files it with the local government. If the borrower does not pay or dispute the notice, the notice of sale is filed to send the property to auction.

A foreclosure will occur when the homeowner defaults on his or her payment obligations. When a negative shock hits the economy, many homeowners will default at the same time, and the fire sale will reduce housing prices even further, hindering residential investment and consumer demand. There is simply an excess supply of houses that cannot be absorbed without prices going down. That being said, a rebound can occur if the amount of houses hitting the market slows down, or if limits to arbitrage/investment are lifted.

After looking at the differences between judicial and non-judicial states, it is clear that it is easier to foreclose a property in a non-judicial state. It is also cheaper and less time-consuming for lenders to foreclose properties in non-judicial states. The foreclosure process in a judicial state is quite expensive, so lenders are discouraged from foreclosing properties. From 2008 to 2009, foreclosure rates in non-judicial states were more than twice as high as the foreclosure rates in judicial states.

To see how different laws in different states affect foreclosure rates, Main *et al.* (2015) looked at ZIP codes close to state borders where the foreclosure law changes. The goal of this analysis was to see if the foreclosure propensity jumps as one crosses the border. The study proved that the ZIP codes on each side of the border are similar except for the foreclosure laws by analyzing a number of different attributes. The analysis looked at ZIP codes within 50 miles of the state border. The authors showed that from 2008 to 2010, there is a large increase in the foreclosure to delinquent account ratio as one moves from a judicial state to a non-judicial state. The difference across borders peaked in 2009, but it fell significantly in 2012 and continued to drop until there was no difference in 2013. The study also considered other possible differences between the states, but it did not find any other patterns.

Observing the difference in house prices, non-judicial states saw a larger drop in house prices during the housing crisis. From 2006 to 2009, the drop was significantly different between non-judicial states and judicial states where prices fell by 43 percent and 28 percent, respectively. Before the recession, there was no evidence of different house price trends between states. As the economy recovered in 2012, there was essentially no difference in house prices between judicial and non-judicial states. The larger drop in house prices was caused by the higher rate of foreclosures in non-judicial states. As more homes foreclosed, there were too many homes on the market for the number of buyers.

House prices dropped more in non-judicial states during the recession, but it is also important to look at how house prices adjusted as the economy recovered. All states saw a similar house price growth from 2009 to 2010, but there was weaker growth from 2010 to 2012 in judicial states. In 2012, non-judicial states experienced a stronger house price recovery. As foreclosures became less common, prices rebounded stronger in non-judicial states.

Across all states, residential investment patterns were similar until 2007. From 2008 to 2009, non-judicial states saw a larger drop in residential investment than judicial states although residential investment slowed nationally. To look at durable consumption, Mian *et al.* (2015) analyzed auto sales between states. There was a smaller decline in auto sales in judicial states. From 2007 to 2009, foreclosure rates can explain 33 percent of the aggregate house price decline and about 20 percent of the residential investment and auto sales decline. The evidence is not as strong as it was for house prices in the recovery period, but non-judicial states also experienced a stronger recovery with auto sales and residential investment in 2012.

Mian *et al.* (2015) used differences in state-specific laws as an instrument to examine the price and real economic effects of foreclosures. With the increase in foreclosures across the country during the recession, there was a huge negative impact on house prices. Since house prices dropped, housing wealth lowered and furthered a drop in durable consumption and residential investment. They found that foreclosures might have been a significant factor in explaining why the recession from 2007 to 2009 was so long and intense. They also looked at what happened after the huge increase in foreclosures. As the number of foreclosures declined after the recession, the difference in foreclosure rates between states disappeared. They also found that non-judicial states experienced a stronger recovery due to fire sales temporarily lowering house prices until new buyers entered the market.

Mian *et al.* (2015) explained that even though foreclosure propensity jumps right at the border, real economic outcomes do not spike the same way. They explained the reason for this through general equilibrium. Even though there are two different states, they both affect the same economy. This concept is directly correlated with Mian and Sufi (2014). Mian and Sufi (2014) used the Creditor and Debtor Island example to explain how what happens if one part of the economy affects all of us.

Overall, Mian *et al.* (2015) are very strong and convincing that foreclosure laws are a strong predictor of foreclosure rates and how foreclosure rates affect house prices and the real economy. One assumption that is tough to accept is assuming that ZIP codes across borders are similar except for foreclosure laws. They analyzed many different aspects of the economies to prove that this is the case. However, there could be other differences between the states not mentioned.

Mian *et al.* (2015) were very in-depth and thorough with respect to the foreclosure process between states and the effects on house prices and the real economy. The study also brought up some other topics that would be worth researching in the future. One possible idea for future research would be to look at the recovery period after the subprime crisis. There could be a study done to see what market frictions were alleviated leading to the recovery, such as any changes in tax code.

## Multiple Choice Questions

1. According to Mian *et al.* (2015), what are the key differences between a judicial and a non-judicial foreclosure state?
   (a) In a non-judicial state, lenders send a notice of default to the borrower
   (b) A judicial state allows the lender to automatically sell a property without going to court when a borrower is delinquent
   (c) The foreclosure process is typically cheaper and faster in a non-judicial state than in a judicial state
   **(d) Both (a) and (c) are true**

**Explanation:** A judicial state requires the lender to sue the borrower in court before they can sell the property. A non-judicial state allows the lender to foreclose the property without going to court as long as they send a notice of default to the borrower. In a non-judicial state, the original mortgage document gives the lender the right to foreclose a property once a borrower is delinquent. Since non-judicial states do not require the lender and borrower to go to court, the foreclosure process in non-judicial states is typically cheaper and faster than the process in a judicial state.

2. According to Mian *et al.* (2015), which of the following jump discretely at the border between a judicial and non-judicial state?
   (a) House prices
   (b) Auto Sales
   **(c) Foreclosure Propensity**
   (d) Residential Investment

**Explanation:** Mian *et al.* (2015) proved that foreclosure propensity jumps between state borders with differing foreclosure laws because laws govern specific states and end at state borders. On the other hand, factors like auto sales and residential investment contribute to the same economy, regardless of state borders. There is a spillover effect between the states since they are so close to each other. The spillover effect is not as significant with house prices, but it is still relevant. While the foreclosure laws differ at the border, the effect from the foreclosures affect house prices nearby regardless of the border.

3. According to Mian *et al.* (2015), in the fire sale model, if participants expected house price growth to eventually recover in non-judicial states, why did house prices fall so dramatically from 2007 to 2009? Why didn't investors or owner–occupiers rush in to buy?
   (a) Slow moving capital
   (b) General equilibrium
   (c) Limits to arbitrage
   **(d) Both (a) and (c) are correct**

**Explanation:** In the fire sale model, the housing price decrease is in direct correlation with the basic economic law of supply. When there is too much of a product, prices will go down. That being said, the simple solution would be to just have investors or arbitrageurs come in and buy the excess supply of houses. But from 2007 to 2009, there was a dramatic decrease in housing prices due to slow moving capital and limits to arbitrage. To be more specific, slow moving capital could mean "investors being unable to gather the capital and expertise to buy and rent out homes during the financial panic." Limits to arbitrage can include not being able to obtain financing to purchase a home. Eventually these limits or frictions in the economy are lifted.

## References

Mian, A., A. Sufi and F. Trebbi (2015), "Foreclosures, House Prices, and the Real Economy", *Kreisman Working Papers Series in Housing Law and Policy* 6.

Mian, A. and A. Sufi (2014), *House of Debt*, The University of Chicago Press.

# Chapter 6

# Political Economy During the Bust

*In collaboration with* Patrick Connolly
and Joseph O'Shasky

The subprime mortgage crisis prompted an unprecedented, and often controversial expansion of the government intervention in the economy. Ben Bernanke was of the belief that if major banks and mortgage lenders were left to die, it would bring down the global economy with them. Was congress right in allowing the government to bail out the banks? To answer this question, one must first uncover if Congress was acting in the best interest of the people.

In 2008, the U.S. Congress passed two of the most significant pieces of federal legislation in U.S. economic history. On July 26, 2008 the American Housing Rescue and Foreclosure Prevention Act (AHRFPA) was enacted by the U.S. Federal Government. This bill provided $300 billion in Federal Housing Administrative insurance, as well as unlimited support of Freddie Mac and Fannie Mae. On October 1, 2008, the Emergency Economic Stabilization Act (EESA) was signed into Congress. This Act allowed the U.S. Treasury department to save failing banks through direct purchase of new equity and afflicted mortgage backed securities in amounts up to $700 billion. These bills have raised the national debt ceiling to over $1 trillion, and have assured significant government intervention in financial industries for years to come.

Mian, Sufi, and Trebbi (2010) discuss the influences of special interest groups, constituents, and political ideologies on economic federal legislation, specifically AHRFPA and EESA. Each voting member of the U.S. Congress has constituents that they are expected to represent in return for their electoral support. Included in these constituent groups are often large financial services firms that donate large amounts of money to campaigns. Upon giving these donations, the firms expect that the politician will take their opinions into account when voting on bills. Financial donations are very controversial topics; Mian, Sufi and Trebbi attempt to explain why congressmen are influenced by these groups and which type of politicians are more likely to vote in favor of their special interest groups. By the end of this essay, the reader should be able to understand the answer to this critical question: How and why was the legislation of the AHRFPA and the EESA influenced by special interest groups, constituents, and the ideologies of congress?

Mian, Sufi and Trebbi filled the analysis with their own opinions, opinions of other renowned economists, and analysis of data and summary statistics. Although there is a copious amount of data in the article, the authors utilized four main sets of data: consumer credit data, congressional electoral and voting data, campaign contribution data, and voter registration data. In order to obtain the consumer credit data, the authors used the reporting agency Equifax. Equifax collects consumer credit reports and aggregates them at the ZIP code level which allows the authors to breakdown particular politicians voting block within a congressional district. The second main data set, congressional electoral and voting data, is comprises party affiliations, vote margins from November 2006, and committee assignments. The campaign contribution data comes from the Center for Responsive Politics (CRP), which is a non-profit organization that collects the information from political contribution reports in the Federal Election Commission. The fourth data set, voter registration data, is composed of the fraction of Republican and Democratic voters for 84 percent of all U.S. Congressional Districts. This data was collected by a political technology firm, Aristotle. Although there are many findings and statistics disclosed in this piece, they were all used to explain the relationship of Constituent Interests with AHRFPA, and the Special Interest Groups with EESA.

In the study of the AHRFPA and the Role of Constituent Interest Groups, the authors used an empirical formula to evaluate the probability a representative is influenced enough by constituent interests and special interest to tilt their vote in favor of the bill. It was found that Democrats voted almost unanimously in favor of the AHRFPA bill, with only 3 out of 236 Democratic Representatives voting against it. Moreover, it was found that 85 of the 233 that voted for the bill had mortgage default rates below the Republican median. Since the democrats almost universally voted in favor of AHRFPA, the authors get into much further detail on the effect of Constituent Interest Groups on Republicans than for Democrats.

"Republicans from higher default rate areas are more likely to vote in favor of the AHRFPA. The effect appears across the distribution and is particularly strong when default rates rise above 7 percent" (Mian, Sufi, and Trebbi). The authors give a graph that plots the mortgage default rate and the propensity to vote in favor. The propensity to vote in favor of AHRFPA is consistent at 0.2 while the default rate is between 0 and 0.07. The propensity to vote in favor jumps from 0.2 to 1.0 between the default rates of 0.07 and 0.12. This proves that almost every Republican Representative is influenced by their constituents when mortgage default rates begin to rise. Moreover, the authors explain that a one-standard deviation increase in default rates leads to a 12.6 percent increase in likelihood of voting in favor of AHRFPA. Campaign contributions by financial services firms have no effect on the voting pattern of Republicans, while having a more conservative ideology reduces the likelihood of voting in favor of the bill.

Since the EESA bill is focused on saving the financial services industry, these firms donated large amounts in exchange for increased influence over politicians. This bill was first rejected on

September 29, when 60 percent of Democrats and only 25 percent of Republicans voted in favor of it. Then, on October 3, 75 percent of Democrats and 45 percent of Republicans voted in favor of the bill which resulted in an enactment. So, how did the special interest constituents influence legislators? And what caused politicians to change their voting decision on October 3, 2008?

Mian, Sufi, and Trebbi propose that "There is a positive relation between the amount of financial service industry campaign contributions received by a politician and the probability of voting for the EESA." It is also noted that party affiliation has no substantial impact on voting patterns. This influence is mostly a result of campaign donations from the financial services industry. In fact, when the votes of the retiring politicians are removed, the correlation between contributions received and probability of voting in favor of EESA is even stronger. Thus, there is a causal relationship of campaign contributions on politicians voting behavior.

Following the failure to pass the EESA bill on September 29, there was the largest intraday percentage decline in stock market value. This economic collapse lead to a mobilization of constituents whose portfolios were negatively affected because they switched their ideologies and were now supporters of direct government involvement. The results show politicians with higher default rates and a higher percentage of constituents working in the financial services industry were more likely to switch votes. Specifically, Democrats with high mortgage default rates and large fraction of constituents with income over $200,000 were more likely to switch votes. For Republicans, the percentage of constituents working in the financial services industry was the most significant determinant of vote switching.

Through their examination and analysis of the data collected, Mian, Sufi, and Trebbi (2010) were able to find strong correlations between politicians voting habits and the interests of their constituents or special interest groups. More specifically, they found that Republican politicians whose constituents had a high level of mortgage default rates were more likely to vote in favor of AHRFPA than Republican politicians representing constituents in an area with lower levels of mortgage default rates. In regards to the passing of the EESA, they found that politicians, in general, were more likely to vote in favor of the act after receiving campaign contributions from financial services industry, the effect of the special interest groups and constituents is smaller for conservative politicians, meaning they were more likely to stick to their political ideologies than liberals.

Mian and Sufi (2014) discuss the effects of the Great Recession and the collapse of the housing bubble. Similar to the findings in Mian, Sufi, and Trebbi (2010), the authors argue that the legislation passed after the housing bubble finally burst was influenced by special interest groups and constituents. According to Mian and Sufi (2014), financial service industries had a tremendous influence on passing legislation after the housing market crash of 2008. Financial service industries had the most to lose after the bubble burst and they did everything in their power to minimize the burden on their shoulders and transfer that burden onto the average U.S. citizen. This included heavily supporting legislative acts that would aide in the bail out of the major financial service industries, effectively saving themselves from the mess that they played a major role in creating.

While the amount of data collected on these topics is substantial, the authors missed out on the opportunity to provide a stronger case as to why so many legislators changed their vote. By conducting further in-depth research, specifically further researching whether there was an increase in campaign contributions after the failure to pass EESA on September 29 or not, the authors would have been able to provide a stronger argument as to how and why the legislations of AHRFPA and EESA were influenced by special interest groups, constituents, and the ideologies of Congress.

## Multiple Choice Questions

1. According to Mian, Sufi, and Trebbi (2010), a Democratic politician who initially voted against the EESA is more likely to

do what, after receiving campaign contributions from special interest groups and their respective constituents than a Republican politician?

(a) Vote against the EESA a second time

**(b) Switch their vote in favor of the EESA**

(c) Retire

(d) None of the above

**Explanation:** The correct answer is (b): According to Mian, Sufi, and Trebbi (2010), the influence to switch their vote in favor of the EESA is mostly a result of campaign donations from the financial services industry. They also state that when you remove the votes of the retiring politicians, the correlation between contributions received and probability of voting in favor of EESA is even stronger. This goes to show that there is a causal relationship of campaign contributions on politicians voting behavior.

2. According to Mian, Sufi, and Trebbi (2010), following the failure to pass the EESA on September 29, 2008, what was most likely the cause of the rapid mobilization of constituents in support of the act?

(a) **The largest intraday percentage decline in stock market value**

(b) Plummeting house prices

(c) Decreasing interest rates

(d) None of the above

**Explanation:** The correct answer is (a): Mian, Sufi, and Trebbi (2010) argue that following the initial failure to pass the EESA, the largest intraday percentage decline in stock market value occurred. Constituents whose portfolios were most negatively affected, tended to switch their ideologies and support direct government involvement. The results show politicians with constituents who were negatively affected and those with constituents working in the financial services industry were more likely to switch votes based on their constituents' new found support of the act.

3. According to Mian, Sufi, and Trebbi (2010), why were Republican representatives from higher default rate areas more likely to vote in favor of the AHRFPA than those in lower default areas?

(a) They were following their own political agenda
(b) They were influenced by special interest groups
**(c) They were influenced by their constituents**
(d) All of the above

**Explanation:** The correct answer is (c): In their article, Main, Sufi, and Trebbi (2010) presented a graph that plots the mortgage default rate and the propensity to vote in favor of AHRFPA. The propensity to vote in favor of AHRFPA is consistent at 0.2 while the default rate is between 0 and 0.07. The propensity to vote in favor jumps from 0.2 to 1.0 between the default rates of 0.07 and 0.12. This proves that almost every Republican representative is influenced by their constituents when mortgage default rates begin to rise.

## References

Mian, A. and A. Sufi (2014), *House of Debt*, USA: The University of Chicago Press.
Mian, A., A. Sufi and F. Trebbi (2010), "The Political Economy of the U.S. Mortgage Default Crisis", *American Economic Review* 100, 1967–1998.

# Chapter 7
# REITs

*In collaboration with* Brian Lauscher
and Eduardo De La Torre

Traditional real estate investment is often criticized for not being as accessible due to its illiquid nature, and because of the risk profile associated with such investment. Real Estate Investment Trusts (REITs) were created in order to provide real estate investment vehicles that were well diversified. Although the subprime mortgage crisis dealt mainly with residential real estate, the externalities that the fall in residential real estate posed on commercial properties, both through direct fall in property values and decreased revenues for commercial businesses, created a vicious contractionary cycle that must not be overlooked. Also, looking at the performance of these REITs in comparison with the underlying properties can help us separate the effects that certain economic factors have on property values.

A quick look at real estate investment trusts during the financial crisis shows that their returns were tremendously volatile during this time period. Between January 2007 and February 2009, the National Association of Real Estate Investment Trusts All Equity REITs Index (NAREIT — an index of all publicly traded REITs) fell nearly 7,000 points from a high of 10,256 — representing a 67 percent decline in the value of the index. Meanwhile, between

September 2008 and February 2009, the National Council of Real Estate Investment Fiduciaries (NCREIF) Property Index (NCREIF — a composite of a large pool of independent real estate properties) fell only 15 percent compared to NAREIT's 60 percent drop. Through these findings, it is evident that REITs declined in price far beyond their underlying property value declines. Sun, Titman, and Twite (2015) make note that the large difference in declines is due to both leverage and financial distress, so they explore both in their analysis.

Consistent with leverage and financial distress costs intensifying the price decline, Sun, Titman, and Twite found that the share prices of REITs with higher debt-to-asset ratios and shorter maturity debt fell more during the 2007 to early-2009 crisis period. Although REIT prices rebounded with the bounce back in commercial real estate prices, financial distress costs had a permanent effect on REIT values. They found that REITs with more debt due during the crisis period tended to sell more property and issue more equity in 2009, when prices were depressed.

The main question that Sun, Titman, and Twite (2015) explore is why REIT prices were so much more volatile during the financial crisis than the underlying commercial real estate. Subsequently, the main goal of Sun, Titman, and Twite (2015) is to uncover an explanation for the impact of financial leverage and financial distress on REIT returns. By looking at the maturity structure of the debt, as well as the debt ratio, they were able to separate the amplification effect of leverage from the effect of financial distress.

Sun, Titman and Twite examined overall REIT returns for two separate time periods; January 2007–February 2009 (when REIT prices collapsed) and March 2009–December 2011 (which is referred to as the rebound period). To further explore the impact of financial distress costs, they examined whether firms with more debt due in 2008 and 2009 made choices that diluted the value of existing shares — how their capital structures influenced how much equity they raised and the extent to which they sold properties during the distress period.

An analysis of the collapse (January 2007–February 2009) reveals that REITs with more leverage experienced the largest price declines. The data show that a one-standard deviation increase in market leverage was associated with a 13.4 percent decrease in cumulative returns. REITs with relatively more short-term debt fell significantly more during this time period — suggesting a significant part of the decline was due to concerns about financial distress costs.

The data showed that larger REITs suffered the largest declines during this time period. A one-standard-deviation increase in total assets is associated with a 9.7 percent decrease in cumulative returns. All property groups across the board experienced a price decline with the extent of the decline varying significantly across groups. The significant differences across property types persisted even with the inclusion of measures for leverage and financial distress.

An analysis of the price rebound period (February 2009–December 2011) showed that size, leverage, and the maturity structure of the REITs influenced the magnitude of the REIT returns during this time period. In this case, a one-standard-deviation increase in market leverage was associated with a 30.8 percent increase in cumulative returns. In their analysis, Sun, Titman and Twite attributed the stronger returns experienced by larger REITs to an overreaction to the negative events in the earlier period.

Finally, performance over the entire time period (January 2007–December 2011) shows that REITs with substantial amounts of debt that matured during the crisis period did ominously worse over the entire time period. This could be because they may have been forced to sell properties or issue equity at unattractive prices, they may have lost key personnel, or they may have been forced to divert their attentions to deal with a financial crunch. Additionally, there was no size effect over the entire REIT and Commercial Real Estate Returns period.

REIT prices reacted more to the financial crisis than the underlying commercial real estate because REITs are leveraged investments — however, leverage cannot explain the entire story of the price fluctuations. The NCREIF index, being based on appraisals, is both slow to react and tends to underreact to major price changes.

NCREIF could also overreact to changes in property prices — this is at least part of the explanation. Values of REITs represent more than just their underlying properties, so it is possible for their values to decline much more than the values of their underlying properties, even after accounting for their debt obligations.

Many of them have large pipelines of development deals as well as platforms that allow them to exploit positive net present value opportunities in the future. It is likely that during the financial crisis the perceived values of those opportunities evaporated or even turned negative — this is only a small part of REIT values, so this effect is small. The riskiness of REITs dramatically increased around the crisis period, causing REIT prices to decline, as required rates of return increased.

Sun, Titman, and Twite (2015) examined the relationship between the proportion of the REIT's total debt due in two or three years from 2006 and the level of equity issues and property sales in 2009. The proportion of debt due in the short-term had a significant influence on the financing and investment decision of REITs following the price decline in 2007 and 2008. In 2009, REITs with relatively more short-term debt in 2006 (i.e. more debt due in two or three years) raised proportionally more equity (both common and preferred stock) and were net sellers of property (i.e. sales exceeded acquisitions).

The overall findings of Sun, Titman, and Twite (2015) show that a significant part of the decline in REIT prices was due to anticipated costs associated with financial distress. Share prices of REITs with higher debt-to-asset ratios fell more during the crisis period, which is consistent with the pure leverage effect. As the data show, the decline was greater for REITs with more variable interest rate debt and more debt coming due in 2008 and 2009. Additionally, the extent of these effects persisted over the full sample period (January 2007–December 2011). Other findings showed that REITs with more debt due in 2008 and 2009 raised relatively more equity capital and sold more properties (i.e. sales exceeded acquisitions).

Sun, Titman, and Twite (2015) have clear ties to Mian and Sufi's (2014) book on the recent financial crisis. In this book, Mian and

Sufi note that "Debt amplifies the decline in asset prices due to fore-closures and by concentrating losses on the indebted ..." (p. 70). This is exactly what Sun, Titman, and Twite found to be true — a high debt-to-asset ratio for REITs led to a larger decline in asset prices. This shows that there are similarities between the effects of leverage in the residential mortgage market and REITs.

Potential problems in Sun, Titman, and Twite (2015) include a high level of cross-sectional dispersion in the second time period — the level of statistical significance is statistically low in their data analysis. Additionally, there is likely to be a tendency of the REITs that are best positioned to cope with the effect of financial leverage to have the highest debt ratios with the shortest maturities. Also, one should pay special attention to the legislation that allowed REITs to substitute stock dividends for cash dividends. This legislation allowed those most exposed to financial distress costs to conserve liquidity, enabling them to mitigate the costs of financial distress; if REITs had been forced to maintain payouts, the robustness of the financial crisis would have been amplified.

Some suggestions for future research are to investigate relation-ship between the real estate cycle and overall business cycle as early as 2006. Betas increased prior to the crisis, but Sun, Titman and Twite do not know what caused this increase. Increase in cost of capital for REITs could have contributed to the downturn. Another suggestion would be to explore the possibility that many of the larger REITs were more levered than was evidenced by their balance sheets. Large REITs declined more than smaller ones in the downturn, but rebounded in the later period. Evidence indicates initial decline was not due to selling by institutional investors.

## Multiple Choice Questions

1. According to Sun, Titman, and Twite (2015), which of the following statement is accurate?
   (a) REIT prices declined more than their underlying real estate asset prices. This is amplified by REITs being unlevered and having short maturity of debt

   (b) REIT prices declined less than their underlying real estate asset prices. This is amplified by REITs being unlevered and having short maturity of debt

   (c) REIT prices declined less than their underlying real estate asset prices. This is amplified by REITs being highly levered and having short maturity of debt

   **(d) REIT prices declined more than their underlying real estate asset prices. This is amplified by REITs being highly levered and having short maturity of debt**

**Explanation:** (d) is the accurate answer because, as Sun, Titman, and Twite (2015) explain, REITs declined more than their underlying asset prices due to high leverage and financial distress of maturing short-term debt. Short-term maturity of debt caused REITs prices to fall because they were forced into early liquidation of assets in a poor seller's market. (a) is incorrect because REITs were levered. (b) is incorrect because REITs declined more than their underlying real estate asset prices and REITs were levered. (c) is incorrect because REITs declined more than their underlying real estate asset prices.

2. According to Sun, Titman, and Twite (2015), the overall findings of the paper show that a significant part of the decline in REIT prices was due to:

   (a) Anticipated costs associated with financial distress

   (b) Anticipated costs associated with levered losses

   (c) Long-term debt

   **(d) Both (a) and (b)**

**Explanation:** (d) is the correct answer because a large part of the slump in REIT prices was due to REITs reaction to financial distress of short-term debt coming due and the amount of leverage REITs had. This financial distress came in the form of increased general administrative expenses and being forced to sell properties at losses. (a) is incorrect because financial distress was only part of the decline. (b) is incorrect because the levered losses framework was only part of the decline. (c) is incorrect because long-term debt was not a main driver of the decline in REIT prices.

3. According to Sun, Titman, and Twite (2015), what is true of REITs debt-to-asset ratio?

   (a) REITs with more debt maturing in 2004–2007 raised relatively more equity capital and sold more properties (sales exceeded acquisitions) in 2009

   **(b) REITs with more debt maturing in 2007–2009 raised relatively more equity capital and sold more properties (sales exceeded acquisitions) in 2009**

   (c) REITs with more debt maturing in 2007–2009 raised relatively less equity capital and sold more properties (sales exceeded acquisitions) in 2009

   (d) REITs with more debt maturing in 2007–2009 raised relatively less equity capital and sold less properties (sales exceeded acquisitions) in 2009

**Explanation:** (b) is correct because REITs with a higher amount of short-term debt maturing in 2007–2009 raised more equity capital and sold more properties in 2009 compared to REITs with lower debt obligations. The reason that REITs with higher short-term debt in this time period sold more properties was because they needed immediate cash to pay off the debt obligations. (a) is incorrect because the time period was in fact 2007–2009. (c) is incorrect because these REITs raised relatively more equity capital. (d) is incorrect because these REITs raised relatively more equity capital and sold more properties in 2009.

## References

Mian, A. and A. Sufi (2014), *House of Debt*, USA: The University of Chicago Press.

Sun, L., S. Titman and G. Twite (2015), "REIT and Commercial Real Estate Returns: A Postmortem of the Financial Crisis", *Real Estate Economics* 43, 8–36.

# Chapter 8

# U.S. Homeownership Rates

*In collaboration with* Emma Shepard
and Jacob Gutierrez

Homeownership increased dramatically as mortgage loans were more widely available, but this was just one aspect of the economic conditions that made owning a home more accessible. Increasing the access to homeownership was one of the main goals the American government pursued beginning in the 1990s. Understanding how factors other than lower underwriting standards affect homeownership rates can help us figure out a more responsible way to reach that goal without the dangers of subprime lending.

The driving question of Gabriel and Rosenthal (2015) is to discover the driver of homeownership rates. Specifically, they focus on the boom and bust of homeownership rates during the decade between 2000 and 2010, and try to decompose the effects of population attributes vs. market conditions and attitudes on these rates.

Gabriel and Rosenthal (2015) primarily used individual-level data from Public Use Micro Areas (PUMAs) gathered by the U.S. Census Bureau in 2000. To supplement this data, they also used data from PUMAs collected by the 2005 and 2009 American Community Services. The data compiled by the 2000 U.S. Census Bureau was based upon a 5 percent sample of the U.S. Population, whereas the latter two surveys were 1 percent samples of the U.S.

population. The data was used to provide age-stratified regression analysis for individuals between the ages of 21 and 89. This was done in order to clearly indicate how certain variables affect home-ownership over the life cycle.

Another way to extrapolate the effects of specific variables on homeownership is by controlling for particular variables. Thus, the data used in Gabriel and Rosenthal (2015) had control variables broken down into four broad types: the first category is demographic controls, the second category is labor-related controls, the third category is geographic control variables, and the fourth category of control variables contains three local housing market attributes.[1] The first housing market attribute is the median value of owner-occupied homes in a specific family's PUMA of residence. The second attribute is the one-year-ahead forecast of the percentage change in quality-adjusted house prices in the household's metropolitan areas. The third local housing market attribute is house price volatility for the metropolitan statistical area in which the household resides.

Gabriel and Rosenthal (2015) examined the theoretical consumption–investment model developed by Henderson and Ioannides in 1983. They thought the main implication of the model was "that any factor that contributes to a household's investment or consumption demand for housing belongs as a control variable in a regression designed to evaluate the propensity of family to own its own home." The coefficients on the control variables used in the model are reduced form in nature and reflect the combined influence of investment and consumption demands for housing.

A distinguishing factor in the investment–consumption model of Henderson and Ioannides (1983) is that house price volatility takes a major role, whereas previously volatility had not been taken into account amongst the standard user cost factors of the relative cost of owning a home. Yet, taking this into account is necessary because house price volatility reduces the investment demand for housing and discourages homeownership.

---

[1] See Luque (2015) for an examination of local and national drivers of housing and real estate activity.

The main results of Gabriel and Rosenthal (2015) were drawn from a three-part analysis of the data. First, age-specific homeownership rates were calculated for each of the sample years. Next, the changes in these rates were decomposed across the survey years. Finally, age groups were pooled together to further decompose changes in U.S. homeownership throughout the decade.

The first part, looking at age-specific homeownership rates for the sample years, finds that overall homeownership rates fell between 2005 and 2009, after hitting their peak in 2005. While this was especially true for younger families, it is observed that homeownership rates fell for every age group between the sample years of 2005 and 2009. Focusing on recent-movers only, there is a decline in the propensity to become homeowners between 2005 and 2009 as well. Although there was a clear trend in looking at the age-specific data, Gabriel and Rosenthal (2015) analyzed the causes of the changes in these rates, using their model, to draw a conclusion on the largest reason for a change in these rates during the decade.

Decomposing these age-specific rates allowed Gabriel and Rosenthal to see if these changes are primarily driven by population attributes (control variables) or market conditions (estimated model coefficients). The population attributes being considered are demographic, labor-related, geographic variables, and local housing market attributes. The market conditions being considered are the investment demand for housing, the consumption demand for housing, and the effect of borrowing constraints. The results of this revealed that socioeconomic and demographic changes over the first half of the decade decreased homeownership, while market conditions increased homeownership during this period. Since the net effect was that rates rose significantly during this period, it was confirmed that market conditions was the factor dramatically driving up rates. Market conditions during the first part of the decade were favorable for investing in housing, which dramatically drove up rates. Looking at the second half of the decade, the model conveys that population attributes have little influence on homeownership rates, while market conditions reduced aggregate homeownership rates. Analyzing the decade as a whole (from 2000 to 2009), population attributes had an overall effect of decreasing homeownership rates while market conditions increased rates over the entire decade — these two factors had a net effect of increased homeownership by 0.7 percent over the decade. More specifically, market conditions can also explain the boom and bust during the former and latter parts (respectively) of the decade. Looking specifically at recent-movers, the "boom" part of the cycle was less dramatic than when looking at the overall population, but the "bust" was much more dramatic. This is concluded to be a result of inertia (families that bought during the boom and didn't move out during the bust).

In conclusion, the majority of the boom and bust of homeownership rates during the broader boom and bust in the financial markets can be attributed to market conditions and attitudes — not population attributes. Looking specifically at price volatility, which increased between 2000 and 2005 and decreased thereafter, it is concluded that households became more risk loving during the boom, and more risk averse during the bust. The results also show that rates are back down at levels that prevailed between 1970 and the mid-1990s, concluding that there is little lasting effect of the homeownership-encouraging policies of recent decades. Lastly, looking forward, the risk adverse attitudes combined with stricter mortgage underwriting policies suggest homeownership levels will not return to their 2005–2006 peaks. A growing observation in the United States is that younger generations are buying homes later than their parents did. It is observed that younger adults are renting later in their lives than previous generations. This raises the concern that homeownership rates could drop even further to levels lower than those that prevailed between 1970 and the mid-1990s. Gabriel and Rosenthal (2015) analyzed this concern using their model as well, and concluded that rates should not continue to drop going forward. Their overall conclusion is that neither the boom nor the bust of homeownership rates should carry lasting effects into the future.

The article relates to Mian and Sufi's (2014) when they discussed the relationship between homeownership and the macroeconomy. While Mian and Sufi (2014) focuses more on the overall housing price bubble and the Great Recession, Gabriel and Rosenthal (2015) focuses on why there was a boom and bust in homeownership rates (which mirrored the boom and bust of housing prices). However, both recognize that homeowners have a greater propensity to consume when they experience capital gains from homeownership due to an increase in housing prices. Increased investment demand for housing (as compared to consumption demand for housing) was a factor in the increase in homeownership between 2000 and 2005. Mian and Sufi (2014), looking at this effect in a larger macro sense, concluded that spending consumption decreased prior to the housing price bubble bursting. This can also be explained by the decrease in homeownership rates prior to the bubble bursting. The decrease in homeownership rates means that consumers were predicting fewer capital gains, therefore decreasing their investment demand for housing, and therefore decreasing overall consumption out of home equity. Gabriel and Rosenthal's (2015) exploration of homeownership rates before and throughout the Great Recession is a perfect supplement to Mian and Sufi's (2014) larger analysis of the Great Recession. Pairing these two analyses, combined with other academic papers, can provides a more in-depth, well-rounded analysis of the Great Recession. Diving deeper into related issues, such as the boom and bust of homeownership rates, forms a greater argument, rather than creating unsupported assumptions.

Although Gabriel and Rosenthal (2015) was very strong in that it was well thought out and the conclusion was supported by the data, there were still a few weaknesses. One of the weaknesses of the paper was the lack of the role attributed to debt in the bust of the housing market. The authors appeared to view debt as an effect of the boom and bust without discussing the possibility that they may have had the order of causality reversed. This would have been an interesting take on the housing market of the 2000s and how it affected the U.S. economy at the time.

For further research it would be interesting to compare and analyze studies with opposing conclusions. Such as academic articles in which the authors had found data supporting the thesis that the housing boom and bust was due to changes in socioeconomic populations and demographic attributes and not market conditions and attitudes. Being able to refute those arguments with facts would produce a compelling argument.

## Multiple Choice Questions

1. According to Gabriel and Rosenthal (2015), changes in which factor had the biggest effect on the boom and the bust of homeownership rates during the 2000s?

   (a) Socioeconomic populations
   (b) Demographic attributes
   **(c) Market conditions and homeowner attitudes**

**Explanation:** The correct answer to the question is (c): Gabriel and Rosenthal (2015) argued that Market conditions had more affect upon the boom and the bust than changes in socioeconomic populations or even changes in demographic attributes. Gabriel and Rosenthal (2005) had determined that the increase in homeownership in the 1990s was largely if not completely due to changes in the socioeconomic population and demographic attributes. In this current paper Gabriel and Rosenthal used the same methods as previous to determine that the opposite conclusion can be made regarding the housing market's boom and subsequent bust during the 2000s.

2. According to Gabriel and Rosenthal (2015), which of the following was **not** one of the four broad categories of control variables used?

   (a) Labor-related variables
   **(b) House price volatility**
   (c) Demographic variables
   (d) Local housing market attributes
   (e) Geographic variables

**Explanation:** One of the major problems of any academic article, experiment, or survey is chance of omitted variable bias. This occurs when a model does not include one or more causal factors.

The implications of this can be over or undercompensating for the effect of other variables. In an attempt to combat this bias, Gabriel and Rosenthal (2015) controlled for 35 different variables in order to extrapolate the data and effectively prove the reasoning behind their conclusion. They broke down their controls into four major groups: demographic variables, labor-related variables, geographic variables, and housing market attributes. Although house price volatility was one of the three major housing market attributes, volatility itself was not one of the four major groups of control types. Thus, the correct answer is (b).

3. According to Gabriel and Rosenthal (2015), which was **not** a factor that can be attributed to increasing the demand for homeownership?

   **(a) House price volatility**
   (b) Increases in prices of homes
   (c) Increases in capital gains
   (d) Increased investment demand

**Explanation:** Housing price volatility is correlated with a decreasing demand for housing prices. Therefore, the answer is (a). Increases in the prices of homes increases the demand for homeownership, because homeowners receive a capital gain, which thus is responsible for increasing their marginal propensity to consume. Investment demand is a factor attributed to increasing homeownership. The increases in investment demand propelled families to increase homeownership rates across the U.S. in order to attempt to cash in on the increasing prices of homes during the housing bubble.

## References

Gabriel, S. A. and S. Rosenthal (2015), "The Boom, the Bust and the Future of Homeownership", *Real Estate Economics* 43, 334–374.

Henderson, J. V. and Y. M. Ioannides (1983), "A Model of Housing Tenure Choice," *American Economic Review* 73, 98–113.

Luque. J. (2015), *Urban Land Economics*, Switzerland: Springer.

Mian, A. and A. Sufi (2014), *House of Debt*, USA: The University of Chicago Press.

# Part II
# Foreclosures

# Chapter 9

# Estimates and Sources of Price Declines

*In collaboration with* Josh Hyatt and Alex Cranfill

It is evident that foreclosed homes pose externalities to the neighborhoods and communities that surround them. If the contrary were true, a crisis such as the subprime mortgage crisis would have been easier to contain. This chapter explores the specific externalities or "spillover effects" that affect communities. Understanding the effect that these externalities have on communities can help us get some useful knowledge on which aspects of those externalities cause the most harm in hopes of being able to contain them in the future.

During the heart of the recession in 2008, foreclosures were widespread across the U.S. A domino effect ensued. Entire neighborhoods of underwater homes went into foreclosure, eventually bringing down Lehman Brothers and the entire U.S. economy. While evidence exists that the crisis began before the downfall of the elite investment bank, this bankruptcy would propel the nation into a full-fledged crisis. However, an important question still remained. What was the reason for the rampant foreclosure spillover effects?

The goal of Annenberg and Kung (2014) is to determine the source of the foreclosure spillover effects. In order to solve this complex problem, first, it needed to be verified that foreclosures do indeed lead to neighborhood price declines. Once that fact was confirmed, Annenberg and Kung investigated the mechanism in which the spillover effect operates. Are neighborhood price declines from foreclosures merely a result of an increase in supply, or are they the outcome of a disamenity effect, where vandalism or crime from the vacant property creates a negative externality for nearby homes, thus decreasing their price? The goal of Annenberg and Kung (2014) is to investigate these questions. The results can lead to a better understanding of how shocks are spatially transmitted through the housing market and can help policy makers make decisions on the appropriate intervention to contain the foreclosure spillover effect.

To improve on the previous academic research, Annenberg and Kung (2014) used listing data (rather than transactions data) to solve the underlying question. The listing data set covers a plethora of residential properties listed for sale, including real estate owned (REO) and non-REO listings in San Francisco, Washington DC, Chicago, and Phoenix from January 2007 to June 2009. In San Francisco, only single-family homes listed for sale on the MLS were examined, while in the other three cities, all home types (condo, single-family, multi-family) were investigated. However, the data does not begin until October 2007 for the latter three cities. Supplemental data from Altos Research provided the addresses, list prices, and some standard housing characteristics for all houses listed in order to infer the initial listing and final delisting date for all properties. These four cities have the largest populations for which there was good quality data available. There are many more listings at any given time than completed transactions. With much more data, it is possible to look at the effects of foreclosures over a much narrower time frame (weekly) as well as in finer geographical detail. Secondly, this data allowed them to observe the dates that both REO and non-REO properties were listed for sale, including the initial listing date and the sale date. By analyzing these specific dates, it was possible to understand the housing market conditions at the time of agreement. Closing dates lag agreement dates, and the increased information provided by the agreement date allowed Annenberg and Keng (2014) to reduce measurement error and bias in estimators which use a before and after comparison.

First, in order to measure if a competitive effect exists, Annenberg and Kung (2014) ran a linear probability model estimating the propensity of nearby sellers to change their list price in the four weeks before, on the week of, or the four weeks following a new REO or non-REO listing. A listing with a low value of "Dist" or distance (the variable measuring this propensity), is more susceptible to new entrants in the market. If a competitive effect exists, sellers with a low value of Dist should be more likely to adjust their list price in response.

Once verified, to estimate the size of the competitive effect, a regression was run measuring the number of REOs at stage $g$ (a variable to describe an input for each stage of the listing process that is measured and compared — e.g. prior to listing, etc.) in the listing process that are close to (or far from) the property as well as the number of non-REO listings at stage $g$ of the listing process that are close to (or far from) the listed property. The Far group is considered equal to 0.33 miles from the foreclosure, and the Close group is within 0.1 miles from the foreclosed property. The price trends across the various listings in the Far group were used as a control group, while any additional price effects in the Close group is considered a foreclosure spillover. Two key assumptions in this equation are that (1) home prices within 0.1 miles of a foreclosure would not be trending differently from home prices within 0.33 miles of a foreclosure in the absence of the foreclosure, and (2) foreclosure spillovers should be stronger for homes within 0.1 miles of a foreclosure relative to homes within 0.33 miles.

To test for a disamenity effect — where foreclosed properties, through neglect and vacancy, create an eyesore or attract vandalism that creates a negative externality for nearby homes — the previous equation is expanded to measure the change in property values by including time intervals well before and after the listing period. Because it is impossible to measure how the maintenance of each property during the foreclosure affects the price decline, Annenberg and Kung (2014) chose to compare the disamenity effect in high density, low value areas vs. low density, high value areas. This separation is motivated by two key considerations: the bank's return to property maintenance may be lower in low-demand areas and that more urban environments are more likely to attract vandalism. Comparing the results from these two groups allowed them to analyze the significance of the disamenity effect.

One of the key findings from Annenberg and Kung (2014) was that four weeks before or four weeks after a new REO listing, sellers are less than likely going to adjust their own list prices. Additionally, the likelihood a seller adjusts their list price increases noticeably in the specific week an REO enters the market. The article identified that almost all of the price adjustments due to an REO entering the market occurred within 0.5 miles of the REO. These results all point to the fact that foreclosures have a definite effect on house prices within neighborhoods.

Changes in prices as a reaction to new REO and non-REO listings can be interpreted as a spillover effect. Annenberg and Kung (2014) found prices would adjust back to normal upon the sale or removal of listing of a foreclosure on the market. The percentage decrease of house price in reaction to an REO/non-REO entering the market was found to be statistically significant, confirming that the spillover effect was due to competition. Also identified was a 2 percent increase in a house's time on the market for each extra REO listing on the market.

Another interesting result from Annenberg and Kung (2014) was that only in high density, low-income areas (where there is frequent damage and vandalism to foreclosures) did there exist a pre-listing price drop of 1.5 percent on foreclosures. Foreclosures experiencing a pre-listing price drop only occurring in high-density, low-income areas, and nowhere else, are strongly indicative of a disamenity effect as opposed to a competitive effect.

From the evidence, one is able to draw a couple of conclusions. First, there was an observable and significant effect of foreclosures on neighborhood housing prices. Second, each new foreclosure listing on the market added extra competitive pressure on local sellers. Also, contributing to this pressure was banks pricing competing homes aggressively below the market rate in order to quickly offload the defaulted asset. Lastly, in areas of high density and low-income population, a disamenity effect contributed to pre-listing spillover.

In order to alleviate some of the price pressures, there are several things the government can do. Annenberg and Kung (2014) provide several recommendations such as reduce the actual number of REO's for sale, or implementing foreclosure prevention policies.

Both Annenberg and Kung (2014) and Mian and Sufi (2014) found that areas tending to be relatively poorer, such as neighborhoods with high density and low property value, were particularly exposed to the falling markets. In area codes with high density and low property value, disamenity effects amplified the magnitude of the spillover effect and decreased the value of many homes. These decreases in property value to poorer homes were felt even more because of the high leverage used to finance the purchase of the home. Also, observed in both publications was the spillover effect that caused the rise in foreclosures due to collapses in housing prices.

One criticism of Annenberg and Kung (2014) was the way it went about discussing foreclosure spillover effects. It was difficult to follow how they broke down the spillover effect and also its causes. Their work could benefit from better clarifications when discussing foreclosure spillover effects.

As briefly mentioned in the final paragraph of Annenberg and Kung (2014), further research on the welfare benefits/consequences of various governmental foreclosure policies could be conducted. While a goal of this chapter was to better understand the spillover effect and assist the government in creating policy, it is still unknown the effects that would result. Understanding the inherent social benefits/consequences resulting from specific statutes would allow policy makers to create an environment that will strike a balance between social welfare and the number of foreclosures to produce the most benefit for society as a whole.

## Multiple Choice Questions

1. According to Annenberg and Kung (2014), which of the following was **not** a reason that Annenberg and Kung expected zero disamenity effect for many foreclosed properties?

   (a) Not all homeowners will neglect their homes once foreclosure becomes imminent

   (b) If homeowners do neglect their homes once foreclosure becomes imminent, not all forms of neglect will directly affect neighboring home prices

   **(c) Visually damaged homes will not cause a price decrease in neighboring homes because it is assumed that once the home becomes occupied again they will fix the damages**

   (d) Banks can and do hire companies that provide property preservation services for foreclosures

**Explanation:** The correct answer to this question is (c): Annenberg and Kung (2014) assumed that not all owners will neglect their homes once foreclosure becomes imminent, and that even if some do, all forms of neglect will not directly affect neighboring property prices. According to their research, many banks also hire companies to preserve their foreclosed properties. However, because home prices are highly dependent on the local market at the time of the listing, they will be vulnerable to the condition of neighboring households. Vandalized homes can create a negative externality in a neighborhood and significantly decrease the values of all of the homes in the area.

2. According to Annenberg and Kung (2014), which is a benefit to examining listing data as opposed to transaction data when researching the spillover effects from foreclosures?

   (a) There are many more listings than completed transactions at a given time

   (b) Closing dates lag agreement dates which will increase measurement error

   (c) With more data, it is possible to analyze data in more precise time frames (weeks)

   **(d) All of the above**

**Explanation:** All of the above (d) is the correct answer to this question. Obviously, there is significantly more listing data than completed transactions at any given time. Because market conditions can change between the agreement date and the actual date of closing, using listing data enable researches to understand the specific market conditions at the time of the agreement. By doing so, Annenberg and Kung (2014) reduced measurement error and bias in an estimate that uses a before and after comparison. With more data, it is also possible to look at the effects of foreclosures over a much narrower time frame and in finer geographical detail.

3. According to Annenberg and Kung (2014), what are the mechanism(s) through which the spillover effect operates?
   (a) The disamenity effect
   (b) The inflation effect
   (c) The competitive effect
   **(d) Answers (a) and (c) are correct**

**Explanation:** Inflation has nothing to do with foreclosure spillover, thus eliminating answer (b) from the possible correct answer. The main mechanism through with spillover effects operated in this time period was the competitive effect. During the price bubble, the housing market saw many foreclosed homes be listed for sale. This increased competition throughout the country, thus causing the spillover effect. Additionally, in specific sectors of the United States, a disamenity effect also contributed to the spillover effect.

## References

Mian, A. and A. Sufi (2014), *House of Debt*, USA: The University of Chicago Press.

Annenberg, E. and E. Kung (2014), "Estimates of the Size and Source of Price Declines Due to Nearby Foreclosures," *American Economic Review* 104, 2527–2551.

# Chapter 10

# Credit Experiences

*In collaboration with* Artur Prusak
and Alec Greenberg

One consequence a homeowner faces if he is forced to foreclose on a property is the credit implications of failing to honor a loan. Namely, credit scores take a huge hit, which in turn makes borrowing more expensive, and in some cases, makes credit inaccessible. Consumers' economic activity is heavily influenced by the cost of borrowing they face. Decreased household spending only exacerbates an economic environment subject to a subprime mortgage crisis. Understanding the implications that foreclosures have on individual credit can help us prevent an economic contraction such as the Great Recession.

Mortgage foreclosures typically have forward bearing consequences on borrowers that extend beyond the day of delinquency. More often than not, the focus of these consequences lies with the neighborhoods that experience pervasive foreclosures and the negative effects that extend beyond the individuals and families that struggle as a result. Whereas there has been ample research done on the causes of expansive mortgage foreclosure, there has not been nearly as much research on the longer-term effects foreclosure has on individual borrowers. Brevoort and Cooper (2013) explore this untouched segment in-depth, and uncover insight into credit consequences for individuals following a foreclosure.

One of the most significant effects to linger beyond foreclosure is an individual's ability to access credit. Failing to uphold to the terms of one's mortgage agreement has a noticeably harmful effect on a person's ability to obtain credit after the fact. For starters, fore-closing on a mortgage delivers a sizable blow to a person's credit score. The lower the credit score, the more difficult the process in getting credit. In the event an individual is approved for some amount of credit, the relative cost of the loan moves in tandem with credit score; the lower the credit score, the more expensive the cost of borrowing. Brevoort and Cooper (2013) found that access to credit becomes limited for a period of time after a foreclosure, irre-spective of the type of economic shock. This suboptimal ability to obtain credit could be an exacerbated issue for a person. The lower credit scores associated with foreclosure could have an impact on future ability to withstand economic shocks. In turn, delinquencies going forward would be much more common and much more likely, holding the individuals' credit score low for an even longer extended period of time. They chose to focus on the credit scores decline that are tied to foreclosure, and subsequently in the years that follow. They examined whether or not individuals' scores returned to pre-delinquency levels, or if their scores remained low for a considerably long period of time. In addition, they looked at how credits scores and credit performance changed for borrowers after experiencing a mortgage foreclosure.

A common assumption with foreclosure rates is that the rate at which properties foreclose is positively correlated with individuals having negative equity in their homes and properties. While it is very common to see foreclosure for property holders with property values under that of their mortgage — "negative equity" — Brevoort and Cooper (2013) found that many of those individuals with nega-tive equity did not go through the foreclosure process. Surprising still, some individuals that had gone through the foreclosure pro-cess *had* equity in their respective properties. This goes against the standard expected notion of a foreclosure case and affects longer-term financial implications of foreclosures, where negative equity in a home is not necessarily indicative of a foreclosure.

Understanding the limitations of using simulations to examine the long-standing effects of foreclosure, Brevoort and Cooper (2013) used real-world data from the Federal Reserve Bank of New York/ Equifax Consumer Credit Panel. This is a large pool of borrowers' credit records, tracked at the individual-level, quarter-by-quarter from Q1 1999 to Q4 2010. The sample used represented over 334,000 individuals whose mortgages entered foreclosure, providing for a holistic view of the larger population of borrowers. The individuals selected had their identities concealed, allowing the authors to study the same individuals' credit experiences over time. They characterized each individual as per their creditworthiness before their respective mortgage became delinquent, and tracked their credit histories beyond that quarter.

In the time preceding a mortgage foreclosure, credit scores decline and most research on the topic has centered on why these scores decline. Brevoort and Cooper (2013) took a unique approach and examined the magnitude of the declines in credit scores across their data sample. One of the challenges posed to the researchers was the fact that models to evaluate credit scores were not ubiquitous across the industry. In this scenario, measuring declines in credit score is difficult and may be inaccurate; a foreclosure may have substantially different effects for individuals with the same credit score pre-foreclosure. As such, the authors focused on actual score declines of anonymous borrowers (vs. using Fair Isaac Corporation (FICO) score simulations) in the quarter before foreclosure and the quarter post-foreclosure. They found that individuals who had higher credit scores in the quarter before mortgage delinquency experienced proportionally larger credit score drops. The implication of this finding is that, practically regardless of a person's pre-delinquency credit score, borrowers were left with subprime-level scores in the quarter following foreclosure. Even the borrowers who had the highest credit scores in the quarter before delinquency, subprime scores after the occurrence became a norm across the board. This, in turn, impacted individuals' ability to access credit. While insightful, the authors focused their research on *for how long* credit scores would remain suboptimal following mortgage delinquency.

Such significant declines in a person's credit score are not necessarily permanent. As per the Fair Credit Reporting Act, information regarding a person's credit delinquencies must be removed from his/her credit record following a period of seven years.[1] As such, it is expected that after seven years, scores should recover. If individuals maintain on-time payments of their bills, and restrict their use of credit, their respective credit scores may even recover in a shorter window than the seven-year threshold allowed through the Fair Credit Reporting Act. Using the real data of borrowers' credit score recoveries, the authors found that *subprime* borrowers were able to return to their pre-foreclosure levels at a *faster* pace than prime borrowers. Subprime borrowers' post-foreclosure credit scores recovered within two or more years. In contrast, most prime borrowers' credit scores did not reach pre-delinquency levels even seven years after the quarter during which foreclosure occurred. Their data showed that more than 60 percent of subprime borrowers had recovered within two years, while only 10 percent of prime borrowers saw their credit scores return to pre-delinquency levels in the same time period. This trend continued well beyond the seven-year mark for prime borrowers; even an entire decade after foreclosure, scores did not recover for roughly 33 percent of prime borrowers.

Brevoort and Cooper (2013) concluded that credit scores could — in theory — recover in a relatively short time frame after a foreclosure. In reality, however, the continuance of the score decline is prevalent and credit scores do not recover as quickly as theory would suggest. Data analyzed showed that these scores remain low relative to individuals' pre-foreclosure scores, and relative to the expected trend the scores are slated for as an entire population of borrowers. This low-level trajectory remains even after information about the foreclosure is removed from borrowers'

---

[1]For more information, see § 605 of the Fair Credit Reporting Act at http://www.consumer.ftc.gov/sites/default/files/articles/pdf/pdf-0111-fair-credit-reporting-act.pdf (last visited October 3, 2015).

records, indicative of the fact that said credit score declines are not simply a consequence of foreclosure itself.

Individuals' persistently low credit scores, even beyond the seven-year limit in place via the Fair Credit Reporting Act, reveals the presence of some other factors impacting credit scores. Brevoort and Cooper (2013) found that performance on individual credit obligations was the most likely cause of these persistently low scores. This is due to the fact that a borrower's payment history is 35 percent of his/her respective FICO score. Both prime and subprime borrowers experienced similar trends across the data sample, to where delinquency rates spiked to almost 100 percent for borrowers 90 or more days late on a credit obligation in the foreclosure-start quarter. In turn, this impacted borrower behavior, where tightened financial conditions further exacerbated credit performance. Credit score recovery appeared to be particularly difficult for prime borrowers, more so than for subprime borrowers. These credit score declines from a mortgage falling to foreclosure were not temporary problems; they persisted for several years.

While research by Brevoort and Cooper (2013) concluded that credit scores sustained a large fall for both subprime and prime borrowers, the author's research into the expansion of the credit supply seemed rather limited. To better improve further research in the topic, it could be insightful to examine the impact of credit supply expansion leading up to spiked delinquency rates and prolonged suboptimal credit scores. Particularly, research by Mian and Sufi (2014) reveals that household debt essentially *doubled* from 2000 to 2007. The impact of such expansive credit accessibility may shed light on whether or not prime borrowers were truly "prime", or whether or not this was a consequence of loosened underwriting criteria leading up to the crisis. Though Brevoort and Cooper (2013) did consider individuals who were seen as prime borrowers — "flawless payment histories" — the basis by which said individuals are predetermined is set by the authors' threshold of zero credit delinquencies six months before foreclosure, plus at least 12 quarters of on-time payments. Perhaps, with increasingly available data, this threshold can be adjusted to better fit the true population of what constituted a 'prime' borrower in the years leading up to the Great Recession. Additionally, it could be impactful to examine the relationship between mortgage-credit growth and income growth. Mian and Sufi (2014) found that the aforementioned criteria became negatively correlated in the years preceding the 2008 financial crisis. Whether or not this is correlated to prolonged credit score declines is inconclusive. Mian and Sufi (2014) shed light on the securitized mortgage market, where credit scores of 620 or greater had a higher probability of mortgages being securitized than those below the 620 threshold. Perhaps, it could be relevant to examine whether or not a securitized mortgage (and subsequent foreclosure) exacerbated the length of time during which credit scores were disproportionately low. Given the available data in the years following the crisis, there may be additional connections to the persistently low credit scores found by Brevoort and Cooper (2013) to reveal why scores remained so low, and what could be done to prevent such challenges in the future.

In addition to reviewing the works of Mian and Sufi (2014), individuals could also examine Molloy and Shan (2011). This study, much like Brevoort and Cooper (2013), is one of few that study the effects foreclosures have on *individuals*. It provides insight on the economic burden brought upon by foreclosure, and whether or not there is an impact on individual housing consumption.[2] As mentioned earlier, this is in stark contrast to the slew of studies undertaken that study negative impacts on neighborhoods and nearby property prices. However, given the limited quantity of literature that is focused on the *individual*-level, opportunities for future research into the niche, individual-level effects of a foreclosure are equally limited. Perhaps, as more data become accessible with time in the wake of the financial crisis, there will be additional studies available to examine in the near future.

The authors provide very insightful, well-supported information on the nature of foreclosure impact on individual borrowers. Considering the limited array of available literature on

---

[2]See Molloy and Shan (2011) for insight into borrowers and households following the foreclosure of a mortgage.

this segment, Brevoort and Cooper (2013) offer an informative perspective on how subprime and prime borrowers were affected by mortgage delinquencies. These long-standing impacts are still prevalent, particularly as evidenced by individuals' credit scores and difficulties in obtaining credit. The relative difficulty that surrounds credit score recovery to pre-foreclosure levels is a continued concern for subprime and prime borrowers alike. Brevoort and Cooper (2013) show that the aforementioned group, however, has been the hardest hit regarding recovery. The various impacts observed may not reflect changes in a debtor's financial circumstances, but instead a change in the borrower's preferences that lead to subsequent delinquency. As Breevort and Cooper (2013) reveal, these explanations are not mutually exclusive; each can affect one another and be causation for one of the other. This long-winded recovery has impacted consumer expenditures, to where overall macroeconomic recovery has slowed relative to recession recoveries in decades past. Nonetheless, the study conclusively showed that while credit scores can theoretically recover after a short period of time following a foreclosure, in practice these scores *do not* recover as quickly as theory would suggest, and prime borrowers endure this prolonged recovery for longer than subprime borrowers.

## Multiple Choice Questions

1. Select the true statement from Brevoort and Cooper (2013).
   (a) Borrowers who default on their credit cards simultaneously with when they stop paying their mortgages will experience *smaller* score declines than borrowers who only default on their mortgage, all else equal
   (b) Borrowers who default on their credit cards simultaneously with when they stop paying their mortgages will experience *equal* score declines than borrowers who only default on their mortgage, all else equal
   **(c) Borrowers who default on their credit cards simultaneously with when they stop paying their mortgages will**

experience larger score declines than borrowers who only default on their mortgage, all else equal

(d) None of the above

**Explanation**: The correct answer is (c). Choices (a) and (b) are both incorrect because those borrowers who are unable to pay for their mortgage(s) are not rewarded for their inabilities to pay. Instead, they face consequence in the form of sizable declines in their credit score. Specifically, the inclusion of credits cards into the equation show the relationship between different credit obligations, and what impact delinquency has. Brevoort and Cooper (2013) found correlation with borrowers failing to pay credit cards and a more severe impact to said borrowers' credit score. In turn, it becomes more difficult for a borrower to return his/her credit score to the desired pre-mortgage delinquency level.

2. Brevoort and Cooper (2013) found that:
   (a) Borrowers with subprime credit scores before mortgage foreclosure were the only demographic to have subprime credit scores in the quarter post-foreclosure
   (b) Borrowers with prime credit scores before mortgage foreclosure were the only demographic to have subprime credit scores in the quarter post-foreclosure
   **(c) Borrowers with subprime and prime credit scores before mortgage foreclosure were the demographics that had subprime credit scores in the quarter post-foreclosure**
   (d) None of the above — borrowers credit scores recovered to prime level following foreclosure

**Explanation**: The correct answer is (c): Borrowers with subprime and prime credit scores before mortgage foreclosure were the demographics that had subprime credit scores in the quarter post-foreclosure. Brevoort and Cooper (2013) reveals that both subprime *and* prime borrowers (as per pre-delinquency credit score levels) experienced subprime credit scores after they foreclosed. This comes directly from the article's research, where there was no easier situation for prime borrowers after foreclosure. Both demographic groups experienced declines to subprime levels post-foreclosure.

3.  Research done by Brevoort and Cooper (2013) showed which of the following:

    (a) Borrowers with lower pre-delinquency credit scores experienced the largest decline in their credit scores in the quarter after mortgage delinquency

    **(b) Borrowers with higher pre-delinquency credit scores experienced the largest decline in their credit scores in the quarter after mortgage delinquency**

    (c) Borrowers with average pre-delinquency credit scores experienced the largest drop in their credit scores in the quarter after mortgage delinquency

    (d) Borrowers experienced equally large declines in credit score in the quarter after mortgage delinquency

**Explanation:** The correct answer is (b): Borrowers with high pre-delinquency credit scores experienced the largest decline in their credit scores in the quarter after mortgage delinquency. Brevoort and Cooper (2013) found that prime borrowers suffered to a higher degree than subprime borrowers. This is especially interesting to consider, given that prime borrowers are much more credit-worthy than subprime borrowers, yet experienced a much more prolonged recovery. The other answer choices are incorrect because subprime borrowers fared better than prime borrowers, average credit score borrowers were not considered in the authors' analyses, and there was not an equal decline across the borrowers.

## References

Brevoort, K. P. and C. R. Cooper (2013), "Foreclosure's Wake: The Credit Experiences of Individuals Following Foreclosure", *Real Estate Economics* 41, 747–792.

Mian, A. and A. Sufi (2014), *House of Debt*, USA: The University of Chicago Press.

Molloy, R. and H. Shan (2011), "The Post-Foreclosure Experience of U.S. Households", *Federal Reserve Board of Governors*.

# Chapter 11

# Forced Sales and House Prices

*In collaboration with* Seth Konner
and Chang Hoi Yan Yanny

Though the fall in housing prices can be attributed to foreclosures, forced sales also had a significant impact on the decline of the housing sector. Taking into consideration the externalities that arise from selling a house at a fire-sale price, it is pertinent to explore the impact that these sales have on the rest of the houses in a neighborhood. We can use this insight to be able to contain economic downturns and market fluctuations.

A couple is thinking about buying their first house in a specific neighborhood. Almost all of the houses are just out of their price range but two of them just foreclosed. They want to find out if these houses will sell at a discount or affect the others around it, so they could purchase one of them. Campbell, Giglio, and Pathak (2011) look at this idea. They use data on house transactions in Massachusetts over a 20-year time period (1987–2009) to find the impact forced sales have on sale price. Their results suggest that houses sold after foreclosure, or around the time to death or bankruptcy had a negative effect on house prices.

The goals of this paper were to find out how the prices were affected for forced sales. This data could then be used to predict future sale prices in forced sales depending on the location, and type of forced sale. Campbell, Giglio, and Pathak (2011) obtained data about all house sales in Massachusetts from 1987 to 2009 from the Warren Group, a real estate and financial services information company. In order to find out which sales were forced, they obtained data about death and bankruptcy filings from Death Master File of the Social Security Administration and Lexis/Nexis. Using this information, names, addresses, and dates were matched to the sales. To determine if the event resulted in the forced sale, a bound of three years was used around the date of the event.

The data were all taken from Massachusetts, so to understand the data effectively, one needs to understand their specific foreclosure laws. Massachusetts has both judicial and non-judicial foreclosures. A judicial foreclosure starts with the lender presenting outstanding debt and reasons for foreclosure in a notice to a court. A non-judicial foreclosure happens without a court intervention and is established by states' individual laws. In both cases, with help from the Sherriff's office, an auction is the first step in a sale. An opening bid is given for a house, meaning that the house will not sell at the public auction unless this bid is reached. An important feature of an auction is that prospective buyers are not permitted to enter the house, which will be one reason why there is a discount in prices for forced sales. When a bid surpasses the opening bid, then the house is sold. This situation represented 18 percent of the data used, while an unsuccessful auction, in which the property was handed to the lender, accounted for 82 percent of the cases in the data.

Throughout the entire data of 82,000 transactions, 6.1 percent were forced of which 3.5 percent were foreclosures, 1.8 percent were deaths, and 0.8 percent were bankruptcies. The actual number of each situation fluctuates throughout the data sample years. For example, there was a bankruptcy reform that increased the cost of personal bankruptcy in 2005. The data showed an increase of bankruptcies until 2005, then a decrease in the occurrence of bankruptcy sales onward.

When looking into foreclosure related sales, they all take place in the years after a foreclosure because a house cannot be sold through foreclosure before the foreclosure occurs. For the data that Campbell, Giglio, and Pathak (2011) used, 85 percent of the forced foreclosure sales happened within the first year, 9.1 percent happened in the second year, and 1.6 percent happened within the third year. This shows that forced sales for foreclosures happen very rapidly. The urgency is explained because lenders want cash back as soon as possible while not being able to focus on up-keeping houses. Because lenders do not have resources to upkeep the houses, the lenders will sell the houses at a loss to gain as much of their initial investment back as possible.

When delving into the type of housing units that are represented in the complete data set, there were three types. They were single-family, multi-family and condominiums. In the data set, 65 percent of transactions were in single-family homes, 11 percent in multi-family homes, and the remaining in condominiums. But when only looking at the forced sales transactions, multi-family forced sales were more common than condominium forced sales, at 20 percent and 17 percent, respectively.

For simple statistics, Campbell, Giglio, and Pathak (2011) saw that the median forced sales price was significantly lower than the median sale price of any houses. The forced sale median was $123,000 and the median house price at $180,000, which showed a significant difference. While this might seem like a large amount, there were many other forces at work. For example, it was a lot more likely that the forced sale took place in a low-income neighborhood, where prices were generally lower and houses are smaller. This gave a good background for Campbell, Giglio, and Pathak (2011) to control for different variables by utilizing hedonic regression in the next step.

Campbell, Giglio, and Pathak (2011) used a static hedonic regression to calculate the average discount in prices caused by a forced sale. They used the census tract-year effects, and other measurements to estimate the average price discount because of a forced sale. The data that was used to estimate these numbers was taken from data on sales mentioned earlier. This regression used the ordinary least squares method. Using this data, they calculated the average discount in sale price for forced sales in the following categories: forced, death young seller, death old seller, bankruptcy, and foreclosure. They also distinguished the differences between those categories with one or two sellers.

Using this regression, Campbell, Giglio, and Pathak (2011) calculated data on what the average sales prices would be. They found out that the average price discount for a forced sale was 18 percent. This means that any forced sale whether it was a death, bankruptcy, or foreclosure averaged an 18 percent decrease in price. When they looked at more specific cases, the average price discount for foreclosures was a whopping 27 percent. This shows that foreclosures were one of the main drivers that lowered the average sale price for all forced transactions. When they separated the estimates into different categories, young deaths, old deaths, and bankruptcies only had a sales discounts of 5.16 percent, 6.67 percent, and 3.44 percent, respectively compared to 27 percent in foreclosures. The difference in old and young sellers in terms of deaths could be explained from a few different reasons. The discount was higher for older deaths sellers because on average they did not maintain their houses as compared to younger death sellers, leading to a larger discount when it sells. Again, if someone was looking to buy a house that was a forced sale, the best deal would be to buy a foreclosed home because the average sales discount on price would be significantly higher than other reasons for forced sales.

When Campbell, Giglio, and Pathak (2011) delved deeper into each category, they had another variable to look at. This was whether the forced sales occurred with one or two sellers. The data showed that on average the price discount was larger for single sellers. Reasons for this included that there was often tension between two sellers and one often would want to hold out longer to try to get the higher sale price. Holding out longer might lead to a higher price but a reason that single sellers sold quickly was that they wanted the cash as soon as possible without any other opinions.

The results of the data showed trends that Campbell, Giglio, and Pathak (2011) discussed. For example, death-related discounts happened primarily because of poor maintenance, especially when the seller was older (70+). In terms of bankruptcy, the discount was unrelated to size, price, or location of house because of the true liquidity effect, in which the sellers need cash as soon as possible. Finally, in the case of foreclosures, the discounts were higher in lower priced areas because of greater threats to crime and vandalism to houses. In these places, the longer someone held onto a house, the more likely problems with it would occur. These were some reasons that explain the data.

The results indicated that the growth of unforced sales price was unpredictable, while the discount of forced sales was higher with larger shares. Based on the previous regression, Campbell, Giglio, and Pathak (2011) estimated the model again taking into account of multiple foreclosures. Different slopes from 99.0th percentile to above 99.9th percentile were used to segment the transactions in order to find out how foreclosure waves affected housing prices. Campbell, Giglio, and Pathak (2011) also used dummy variables (also known as indicator variables) for previous sales that took place within the year before the current sale (e.g. one to three years before current sale). The value of the variable indicated the absence or presence of the data used during regression. By doing this, they were able to separate the transactions into close and far distances.

The results indicated that only 8 percent of transactions had foreclosures for close (within 0.1 miles) during the year before the sale, while nearly 20 percent of them had foreclosures for far (within 0.25 miles). In addition, geometric average price has been calculated within 0.25 miles to compare with the local foreclosure indicator. Campbell, Giglio, and Pathak (2011) showed that foreclosures predicted lower prices for close houses and the effect was larger in the extreme cases. This showed that if a foreclosure happened close to a forced sale house, then the sellers could experience a drop in price.

Furthermore, the difference of coefficients and implied standard errors has been reported respectively, which were negative consistently. The spillover estimates of foreclosures showed that foreclosure which occurred in 0.05 miles away reduced the housing price within that distance by about 1 percent. A possible reason for this could be explained because an appraiser would look at nearby house prices in determining one's own price.

This essay can be related to the Mian and Sufi (2014). Mian and Sufi (2014) argued that the increase in debt was the primary reason for the financial collapse of the economy. In this way, many people bought houses that they could not afford, and therefore when there was a shock to the economy, many foreclosed on houses or went into bankruptcy. This problem then affected in house sales, and prices in neighborhoods. This is where Campbell, Giglio, and Pathak (2011) data and conclusions link in with Mian and Sufi (2014), who showed how these forced sales had an effect on neighborhood prices as well as prices on sales of the bankrupt and foreclosed home sales. Home prices dropped significantly and a driver behind this was forced sales and the discounts that came along with them.

While this paper showed lots of great information and conclusions, there were some weaknesses that were present. One of the possible problems with the results of this regression was that there might be forced indicators that were correlated with the other variables, which were not included in the model, giving biased results. In addition, the financial crisis might affect the accuracy of the data. The future of forced sales data might be very different because of the economic state of the U.S. going forward.

When thinking about the future, there are many opportunities for future research about the topic. While all of this information came from Massachusetts, it would be very interesting to look at data from different parts of the country. This might show other results and might change the conclusions discussed.

## Multiple Choice Questions

1. According to Campbell, Giglio, and Pathak (2011), there is a forced sale price discount because …
   (a) Lenders do not have skills or capital to maintain empty real estate
   (b) Houses may be in disrepair

(c) There may be an immediate need for cash from the seller
**(d) All of the above**
(e) None of the above

**Explanation:** The answer is (d) because all of the answers are possible. Many houses go into foreclosure as the lenders who receive the house as collateral cannot maintain it. It will be sold immediately for discount because time is needed to find the person who values it the most. For death-related sales, many of the previous occupants might be less inclined to upkeep house because they are unable or unwilling. And finally, in the case of bankruptcy, individuals might need capital to pay off debts, so they do not have time to go through long process of sale.

2. According to Campbell, Giglio, and Pathak (2011), when a forced sale occurs, in general what is the resulting price impact?
   (a) There will be a price premium
   **(b) There will be a price discount**
   (c) There will be no effect on price
   (d) There can be price fluctuation
   (e) The price will be exactly equal to $100,000

**Explanation:** The answer is (b): Forced sales happen for one of the three reasons. It can be foreclosure, death, or bankruptcy. All of these options are bad circumstances where whoever ends up with the property, being the lender, the occupant or the stated person in the will, will want to trade this property for something they can use....cash. None of these people have skills or need to keep up empty house. It will be sold at a discount for reasons including need for cash, state of disrepair, or being unable to inspect home.

3. What is the reason Campbell, Giglio, and Pathak (2011) suggest that causes foreclosure discounts?
   (a) Poor maintenance of the houses
   (b) Urgency of sales
   **(c) Vandalism**
   (d) All of the above
   (e) None of the above

**Explanation:** The answer is (c): Campbell suggested that poor maintenance is the reason for a death-related discount, while bankruptcy-related discounts are caused by urgency of sales immediately after bankruptcy. For foreclosure, discounts are related to vandalism, through two channels. The houses may be damaged already before selling. Also, mortgage lenders have fixed costs so as to protect foreclosed houses. Thus, the cost of protection and the threat of vandalism is higher and larger in low-priced houses and low-priced census tracts.

## References

Campbell, J., S. Giglio, and P. Pathak (2011), "Forced Sales and House Prices" *American Economic Review* 101, 2108–2131.

Mian, A. and A. Sufi (2014), *House of Debt*, USA: The University of Chicago Press.

# Chapter 12

# Contagion in Housing Markets

*In collaboration with* Ish Goomar and Adam Schenck

Foreclosed homes that create a negative externality on surrounding house prices can attribute this fall in value to the impact foreclosed homes have on the comparable valuation approach. If homes in the neighborhood are foreclosed and subsequently sell for prices well below their original value, this brings down the price of all similar homes in the area. This, however, is not the only factor that causes a fall in home values. Externalities such as the appearance of a neighborhood with empty foreclosed homes, or the diminished social value of a city also induce a decrease in home prices. Understanding how these externalities function can help us gain insight into how we can internalize these externalities and reduce the negative spillover effects they project into communities.

The U.S. housing market during 2007 and 2008 took a turn for the worse when housing prices started to collapse. This decrease in household wealth led to an increase in foreclosures. Harding, Rosenblatt, and Yao (2009) argue that foreclosed homes act as a negative externality to other homes in the vicinity. They use statistical methods in order to achieve results supporting their argument. They also take into account that foreclosures may lower the prices of nearby homes for a multitude of reasons. The first reason

they mention is that foreclosures lead to a negative visual externality since the property may be abandoned or vandalized. Another
mechanism may be the social interaction aspect.

The goal of Harding, Rosenblatt, and Yao (2009) is to determine
whether the foreclosures are just a result of general price declines
in the market or whether they cause incremental declines to nearby
homes. They use several different methods to prove their argument. They also divide the paper into different sections in order to
organize their argument for those reading the paper. The sections
are as follows: methodology, data, cumulative effect of multiple
nearby foreclosures, and robustness tests.

For methodology, the researchers first express the price of a
house as a function of the vector of characteristics and market-
determined prices of those characteristics. One characteristic, for
example, may be the presence of nearby foreclosures. Shadow
prices are determined by creating a regression using the observed
characteristics of the homes on house prices. Harding, Rosenblatt,
and Yao (2009) noted that there may be a problem since there are
many unobserved characteristics with homes, such as local trends
in housing prices. They use a vector to split the overall characteristic variable. Harding, Rosenblatt, and Yao (2009) expand their equation to further include a repeat sales model. The repeat sales model
was originally derived from Bailey, Muth, and Nourse (1963) and
Case and Shiller (1989) and allows a way to estimate the trend in
prices and contagion effect of nearby foreclosed properties. This
model now accounts for the rate of price appreciation over and
simplifies the estimation of the model because both observed and
unobserved characteristics remain constant between the sales over
time. The final equation consists of the unobserved characteristics,
the observed characteristics, the overall market price level, and an
adjustment term for nearby foreclosures. The researchers used various methods in order to screen for inconsistencies.

Harding, Rosenblatt, and Yao (2009) needed to identify large
local markets with a large sample of repeat sales. This helps over-
coming the issue of omitted variables described earlier. They also
needed to identify all nearby foreclosures and specifically needed

the latitudes and longitudes of the properties, the foreclosure, and the sale date after the foreclosure. A large proprietary mortgage database was used. They added to the database since many sub-prime mortgages were not included in the initial database. Geographic areas were limited to those where they had the most coverage. They made sure that the purchase transaction data accounted for at least 80 percent of the known foreclosure sales for a particular ZIP code. Initially, 296 ZIP codes met this criteria; after eliminating outliers and unnecessary information, they were left with 140 ZIP codes. The final step in building the database was to geo-code all the properties so that nearby foreclosures could be identified. The foreclosures were categorized into different sections specifying the distance of the foreclosure property. The rings were: (1) 0–300 feet (Ring 1); (2) 300–500 feet (Ring 2); (3) 500–1,000 feet (Ring 3) and (4) 1,000–2,000 feet (Ring 4). The first and second rings include foreclosures very near or on the same block. The latter rings are foreclosures in the same neighborhood that may affect buyer perception of the subject neighborhood. The foreclosures were also categorized by phase of foreclosure. The metropolitan statistical areas were further limited to seven, each with at least 7,500 repeat sales to ensure a proper sample.

The results show that there were significant negative externality effects if there were foreclosures nearby. Foreclosed properties near a subject property cause a decline of 1 percent per distressed property. The contagion amount decreases greatly with distance. This means that there is less of a decline in property values if foreclosed properties are farther away. The effect of a foreclosed property 300–500 feet away is about half that of an immediate neighbor. It was also found that the time where the effect of the negative externality is greatest occurs near the time of foreclosure sale.

Harding, Rosenblatt, and Yao (2009) support publicly funded efforts to reduce the foreclosure issue. They cite that their results yielded estimates lower to what they initially hypothesized. Since significant negative externalities are present with immediate neighbors, significant contagion effects would only affect three to five million homes instead of the earlier estimate of 40 million homes.

They cite the best way to reduce the contagion effect would be to speed up the foreclosure process since the greatest negative effect is the period when the lender needs to take control of the property.

Foreclosure has been shown to have a negative impact on the market price of nearby non-distressed properties. At a rate of roughly 1 percent per distressed property within 300 feet of a non-distressed subject property and decreasing with distance, nearby foreclosure has a negative contagion effect on neighboring properties market value. By using the repeat sales methodology to study housing prices, the authors found that decreasing home values in areas with foreclosures can be directly connected to properties in the process of foreclosing and is not just an overall decreasing trend in nearby property costs. Harding, Rosenblatt, and Yao (2009) also discovered that the negative externality effect changes depending on the phase of foreclosure a distressed property is currently in, with the effect highest at the time of the foreclosure sale and increasing the fastest during the time in which the lender is resuming control of the property from the defaulted borrower. The results pertaining to the severity of foreclosure on nearby housing values were significantly less than previously estimated figures. Given the data, they concluded that the best way to reduce the contagion effect on nearby properties is to accelerate the pace at which the distressed property goes from inevitable foreclosure to lender controlled resale condition.

Mian and Sufi (2014) also discuss the effect of foreclosure on nearby property values in *House of Debt*. While Harding, Rosenblatt, and Yao (2009) argue that decreasing the length of the foreclosure process is one way to lower the costs of the contagion effect, Mian and Sufi (2014) strongly disagree. Mian and Sufi concluded, with the assistance of research done by Francesco Trebbi, that post-2006, house prices fell much more in states with easier and shorter foreclosure processes than those of longer and more complex ones. They found that states that require a court process to evict delinquent borrowers from a property had a market property value decrease of 25 percent, compared to those states not requiring judicial process in which values decreased upwards of 40 percent. This is in direct contradiction to the analysis done by Harding,

Rosenblatt, and Yao (2009) and clearly shows that decreasing the time needed to complete the foreclosure process results in a higher decrease in home market values of nearby properties. According to Mian and Sufi (2014), the reason foreclosure has a negative impact on nearby housing values is due directly to fire sales. A fire sale is when a lender sells a foreclosed property at a very low price so they can quickly recoup the money owed to them by the borrower. When the lender sells a property at a greatly discounted price, it lowers the value of all nearby houses because when a nearby property is being evaluated for its value, house prices around that subject property have a large influence on that property's value due to average neighborhood home value. So when you have a neighborhood filled with houses in the $150–200k range and then a house in that neighborhood is foreclosed and sold immediately at a price of $100k, it lowers the overall value of the neighborhood which lowers the price of the individual properties in the neighborhood. While it seems like minimizing the time a distressed property is visually unappealing would help lower the contagion effect of foreclosure on nearby homes, according to the research done by Mian, Sufi, and Trebbi (2012), they believe that it increases the negative externality due to majorly discounted fire sales.

The original data used in the article comes from a proprietary mortgage database from 1989 to 2007, augmented with purchased data from vendors of housing transactions. This data includes information on home purchase and sale transactions, outcomes of mortgages, and foreclosure and real estate owned (REO) sale information. Harding, Rosenblatt, and Yao (2009) believe that this information can be used to identify the effects of foreclosures on nearby non-distressed property values. One major flaw in this data is that the primary mortgage database does not contain information on a large majority of subprime mortgages, and the purchased data does not include full foreclosure data in all of its regions. This means that the data does not have all the information needed to make detailed analysis of foreclosure effects in all of the recorded areas, forcing the researchers to limit their amount of data to areas including all the information they need to make accurate analyses. A smaller sample size is less accurate than a larger sample size, so restricting the areas that can be analyzed equates to a less accurate conclusion.

With data ranging from year 1989 to 2007, it covers a large period of time. Using data from such a broad time frame does not always mean more accurate results. Over time, trends and patterns change, so a common real estate trends in 1993 may be drastically opposite of the common real estate trends in 2005. This may lead to a skewed analysis when attempting to identify a present trend that may have not been the same over the entire sample period. Also, because the data used in the article is only up to 2007, there is no way for someone to say that the analysis of the sample data is still relevant in today's market. It would be more accurate to identify a trend existing for a shorter sample period than that of one spanning a longer period of time. The article may have been more accurate if they would have attempted to analyze if there was a contagion effect from 2005 to 2007.

Harding, Rosenblatt, and Yao (2009) leave room for possible future research on the topic, such as identifying if the contagion effect is the same for all socio-economic areas. By using data from a more diverse range of socio-economic cities, they could attempt to identify if the externality effect is the same among all classes of neighborhoods. Another possible research analyses could attempt to conclude if the size of the city has an influence on the contagion effect. The data used in the article comes mainly from larger cities and not smaller rural communities. Any research regarding the effect of a variable on the contagion effect can be conducted now that there is some sort of research to compare it to.

## Multiple Choice Questions

1. According to Harding, Rosenblatt, and Yao (2009), which of the following is the most effective way to reduce the contagion associated costs in an inevitable foreclosure?
   (a) Lengthen the period between foreclosure and REO sale
   (b) Delay the foreclosure process
   **(c) Accelerate the foreclosure process**
   (d) Resell the foreclosed property at a discounted price

**Explanation:** The correct answer to the question is (c): One of the main findings of the analysis was the correlation between phase in the foreclosure process and the severity of the contagion effect. The phase that correlated with the greatest increase in the externality was the period between inevitable foreclosure and re-control of the property by the lender. This suggests that the longer the property is between delinquency and foreclosure sale, the more time the effect has to grow, therefore shortening the length of that phase will reduce the time in which the level is increasing equating to a reduction in costs associated with the effect.

2. According to the article, which of the following characteristics associated with a foreclosing property are most responsible for a negative impact on a neighboring home's value?

   (a) Property neglect
   (b) Borrower's reason for defaulting
   (c) Uncertainty of future owner
   **(d) Both (a) and (c)**

**Explanation:** The correct answer is (d): Harding, Rosenblatt, and Yao (2009) concluded that the contagion effect greatly diminished with distance from a foreclosure. Difference in the patterns of effects from a foreclosed property 300 feet from a non-distressed home and that of one 500 feet from a non-distressed home can be interpreted as suggesting that property neglect and uncertainty about future owners are the attributes responsible for the negative effect of foreclosure on neighboring home values. The two main differences were that the further the house was from a foreclosure, the less rapid the contagion discount grew during the delinquency phase, and that the discount is greatest at the time of the REO sale by the lender. They also found that the time at which the negative externality is peak is around the time of the foreclosure sale, with the effect dying down and stabilizing in the period between foreclosure and REO sale, in which the lender is refurbishing the property and placing it on the market. This suggests that lack of maintenance is a key player in the contagion effect.

3. According to Harding, Rosenblatt, and Yao (2009), their analysis suggests that the number of nearby houses significantly affected by a foreclosure is _____ the number thought to have been affected according to previous estimates.

    (a) Double
    **(b) Less than**
    (c) Equal to
    (d) Triple

**Explanation:** The correct answer to this question is (b): According to the authors' findings, the contagion effect is much less than what was previously estimated in past studies. According to the article, a million foreclosures would roughly affect three to five million homes. Previous estimates suggested that a million foreclosures would significantly impact upwards of 40 million homes. The significance of the negative externality created by foreclosed properties is marginal compared to previous estimates. In this article, the researchers found that the negative externality effect is only 1 percent per distressed property for those within 300 feet of the subject property, diminishing to 0.5 percent for those within 500 feet and decreasing even more from 500+ feet away from the subject property.

## References

Bailey, M. J., R. F. Muth and H. O. Nourse (1963), "A Regression Model for Real Estate Price Index Construction", *Journal of the American Statistical Association* 58, 933–942.

Harding, J. P., E. Rosenblatt and V. W. Yao (2009), "The Contagion Effect of Foreclosed Properties", *Journal of Urban Economics* 66, 164–178.

Mian, A. and A. Sufi (2015), *House of Debt*, USA: The University of Chicago Press.

Mian, A., A. Sufi and F. Trebbi (2012), "Foreclosures, House Prices, and the Real Economy", *The Nation Bureau of Economic Research, NBER Working Paper No.* 16685.

# Chapter 13

# Supply or Disamenity?

*In collaboration with* Joe Ferguson, Craig Meister
and Andrew Schramm

Home prices are affected by different economic factors, and often times a series of factors end up creating a vicious, repetitive cycle that lowers housing prices dramatically. Because actors react to incentives, and those reactions create incentives of their own for other actors, it is useful to separate the effects of each economic factor and isolate their effects. This, in turn, allows us to pin-point the root cause, or biggest contributor of the house price decline that happened as a result of the subprime mortgage crisis.

Throughout the late 2000s, as foreclosure rates increased, the price of both single-family and multi-family homes decreased. The question is, by how much is a home's price affected by a foreclosure in its area? Specifically, by looking at an urban area with many homes, one could take a foreclosure in a dense area and witness the effect it has on homes within a small radius. Additionally, there are multiple mechanisms through which a foreclosure can impact the prices of nearby homes. One could assume that as a foreclosed home returns to the market and increases the number of homes that are available in the area it causes a price change. Additionally, the idea that foreclosed homes can be poorly maintained or vacated and will have a negative effect on the price of property in its area.

Hartley (2014) attempts to find a quantitative result for the effects of foreclosures on house prices and argues that there are multiple mechanisms that have different effects when it comes to the price of property.

Utilizing a method of quantitative analysis, this article aims to estimate the effect of residential foreclosures on home values in the area. Hartley (2014) believes there is an externality caused by residential foreclosures. To explore this, he breaks the externality or "spillover effect" into two parts. First, a foreclosure adds an additional unit of housing to the market creating an excess in supply. Second, disamenity of a property caused by deferred maintenance or vacancy will have an effect on surrounding residential property values. For the purpose of this study, the effects on single-family housing and multi-family housing are examined separately. Hartley (2014) estimates the effects of single-family home foreclosures on single-family property values, as well as, multi-family apartment building foreclosures on single-family property values.

The data used by the author comes from several sources. To study residential property sales and foreclosure data of the city of Chicago, he uses data from a private data provision company called Record Information Services. The foreclosure data used in this study is mainly the filing date of the foreclosure, as opposed to the auction date. Next, he collects data from the Cook County Tax Assessor's Office to study individual property characteristics and homeowner tax exemption claim data. These two sources allow for the linkage to be made between foreclosure and sale data to property characteristic data. The author uses geocoding to locate property addresses and calculate the distance between properties and every sale or foreclosure. The sample of this study is all single-family residential property transactions in the city of Chicago from January 2000 to May 2011.

Hartley (2014) uses a fairly simple but intuitive model to calculate the effects of foreclosure on homes. However, he makes three assumptions in order for his results to be considered correct. The first is that the supply of single-family homes is not affected by a foreclosure on a multi-family home. This segmentation is assumed because single families in the market for a home are unlikely to substitute their preferences for a multi-family home. Additionally, it is difficult for multi-family homes to be converted into single-family homes quickly. The second assumption states that the disamenity effect on single-family homes comes from both single and multi-family homes. This assumption is due to the fact that both single and multi-family homes may be subject to deferred maintenance or vacancy after they are foreclosed upon. The third and final assumption states that the disamenity effect created by a multi-family building being foreclosed upon is able to be compared to the disamenity effect that can be created from the foreclosure of a single-family building. This assumption is used so that a multi-family home disamenity effect can be quantified using the number of units in the building and then compared back to the disamenity effect from a single-family building.

Using these three assumptions, Hartley (2014) develops his model to first calculate the effect on the price of a single-family home by the foreclosure of one single-family home and the effect from the foreclosure of a multi-family building containing $N$ units. In this case, the single-family effect is equal to the supply effect plus the disamenity effect and the multi-family effect, multiplied by $N$ units in the building, is equal to $N$ times the disamenity effect per unit. Next, the author calculates the price effect from a multi-family building foreclosure on a single-family home using integrated markets. In this case, the price effect proportional to the $N$ units is equal to the supply effect plus $N$ times the disamenity effect. The effect from a single-family home stays the same as before.

In order to truly understand the effects of residential foreclosure, Hartley (2014) uses controls in his work to adjust for shocks to the economy at the local level and for seasonality. The main finding of his research is that foreclosures in all of the ranges of distance accounted for correlate with a decrease in home prices. Additionally, the price drop is more significant the closer that the property is located to the foreclosure. Moreover, every foreclosure within 0.05 miles is linked to a 0.3 percent fall in prices of single-family homes.

Additional results from this research suggest that the assumptions made about properties of the same type have supply and disamenity implications. Plus, properties that have been foreclosed that have relatively higher values are brought to auction by banks much faster than other properties. Lastly, Hartley's research found that multi-family building foreclosures and single-family home values are not correlated.

Economists must study the spillover effects of residential mortgage foreclosures in order to better understand our housing market. Hartley (2014) concludes that foreclosure spillover effects can be divided into two unique mechanisms; supply shock mechanisms and disamenity mechanisms. After controlling for economic shock outliers and extreme variation in housing prices, the author finds that each single-family foreclosure within 0.05 miles is associated with a 1.3 percent drop in single-family housing prices. In contrast, the foreclosures of multi-family buildings are not associated with drops in nearby single-family home values. In all, the supply effect of foreclosures on nearby homes is roughly a 1.2 percent drop in value per nearby foreclosure with a disamenity effect of about zero.

The article by Hartley (2014) has some relations to the ideas presented in Mian and Sufi (2014). One of the points made by Mian and Sufi is that the location of a foreclosure is important when looking at what properties will be affected. When discussing fire sales, they note that specifically houses around the property subject to the fire sale are the ones that have their price affected the most. This is relatable to the results found in Hartley's (2014) article. Hartley focuses on how properties within a small radius of the foreclosure are affected more than properties that lie further away from the foreclosure. While Mian and Sufi do not discuss the particular pipelines through which house prices decrease that Hartley uses, Mian and Sufi's text arrives at a similar conclusion. The closer in proximity a property is to a foreclosure, the greater the effect of that foreclosure will be.

Hartley (2014) overall, displays a sound argument supported by data; however, there are a few weaknesses that ought to be addressed. First, the assumption that multi-family housing and single-family housing are not substitutes is suspect. This assumption suggests that those seeking single-family would not opt for a unit in a multi-family residence. Given the quantitative nature of the overall argument being made in this paper, one would hope for a more quantitative narrative regarding multi-family/single-family substitution. Secondly, according to Hartley's findings there is no statistically significant correlation between disamenity and home value. It would be beneficial for this study if Hartley were to explore the rationale behind the lacking effect on price in regard to disamenity, as he suspected there a correlation would exist.

With falling housing prices and foreclosure rates, the spillover effects of foreclosures can have a big impact on our market. In future research, it would be interesting to look at the effects foreclosures have in other cities of different population sizes and demographics. In addition, it could be beneficial to look into why the foreclosures of multi-family housing units have little to no effect on surrounding home values. Understanding why the foreclosures of single-family and multi-family buildings affect housing prices differently could assist in pinpointing why prices fall near single-family foreclosures. If the causes of falling housing prices near single-family foreclosures are known, steps can be made to reduce and possibly eliminate the decreased housing prices following a foreclosure.

## Multiple Choice Questions

1. According to Hartley (2014) which of the following is true about building foreclosures and nearby single-family home values?
   (a) Each multi-family building foreclosure within 0.05 miles is associated with a 1.3 percent drop in nearby single-family home values
   (b) Each single-family building foreclosure within 0.05 miles is associated with a 1.3 percent increase in nearby single-family home values
   (c) Both single-family and multi-family building foreclosures are associated with a 1.3 percent drop in nearby single-family home values
   (d) **There is little to no effect of multi-family building foreclosures on nearby single-family home values**

**Explanation:** The correct answer is (d): Answer (a) is incorrect because each single-family building foreclosure within 0.05 miles is associated with a 1.3 percent drop in nearby single-family home values. Answer (b) is incorrect because single-family building foreclosures cause a 1.3 percent drop in surrounding housing prices, not an increase. Answer (c) is incorrect because only single-family building foreclosures affect surrounding single-family house values. Answer (d) is correct. "On a per-unit basis, multi-family building foreclosures are not associated with drops in nearby single-family home values" (Hartley, 2014).

2. What assumption(s) are made by Hartley (2014) in order for his model on housing prices to be appropriate?

   (a) Disamenity effects from single-family and multi-family homes are comparable
   (b) Foreclosure on a multi-family building does not affect the supply of single-family homes
   (c) Disamenity from both single and multi-family homes affect the price of single-family homes
   **(d) All of the above**

**Explanation:** The correct answer is (d): All three of these assumptions are necessary for Hartley's (2014) model. The disamenity effects from both types of homes are comparable because the per unit effect from a multi-family building must be used to relate back to the effect brought on from the foreclosure of a single-family unit. The author assumes that a multi-family building being foreclosed upon will not have a supply effect on single-family homes because buyers of single-family property will not substitute for multi-family homes and the multi-family homes cannot be converted into single-family homes quickly. Finally, the author assumes that the disamenity effect of both types of housing affect the price of single-family houses. This is because vacancy and/or deferred maintenance can affect local property of different types.

3. Which of the following is true according to the Hartley's (2014) study about residential foreclosures?

   **(a) The further a property is from a foreclosure, the greater the price impact will be**
   (b) The further a property is from a foreclosure, the lesser the price impact will be
   (c) Foreclosures generally have a greater impact on prices from disamenity than excess supply
   (d) Just answers (b) and (c)

**Explanation:** The correct answer is (a): The proximity to a foreclosure definitely has an impact on the extent to which a given property realizes a price impact. Hartley (2014, p. 113). concludes that, "The magnitude of the estimates drops almost monotonically as the distance to the foreclosures increases." This is saying that the closer a property is to a foreclosed home, the greater the impact on price for that nearby property. The effect that a foreclosure has on nearby properties is independent of the characteristics of that property. An otherwise valuable property loses its value simply because a nearby property defaulted/foreclosed.

## References

Hartley, D. (2014), "The Effect of Foreclosures on Nearby Housing Prices: Supply or Dis-amenity?", *Regional Science and Urban Economics* 49, 108–117.

Mian, A. and A. Sufi (2014), *House of Debt*, USA: The University of Chicago Press.

# Chapter 14
# Post-foreclosure Experiences

*In collaboration with* T. J. Dragotta and Nick Malpede

Foreclosures can be a catastrophic experience for households. Aside from the experience of losing the physical asset that is a home, households must also deal with the repercussions that are caused by defaulting on a mortgage. The destruction that a foreclosure leaves behind is reflected in the loss of wealth as well as the negative implications it has on individuals' credit scores. It is important to understand what households must face after experiencing a foreclosure, as consumer behavior is greatly affected.

Throughout the history of the United States, there have been countless studies regarding the financial crises that have hit the economy. The Great Depression, the Dot Com Bubble, and the Great Recession are all examples of these trials. Economists spend hours and hours studying these economic downturns. However, the majority of the analyses regarding these events only tell one of side of the story. The emphasis on these studies has been on what has caused these periods of economic turmoil, as well as how we can prevent them in the future. The other side of the story is, how individuals react to these events is of equal importance to the well-being of the country's economy. An understanding of how households adjust in the face of financial adversity better prepares the country for dealing with these seemingly recurring instances.

The goals of Molloy and Shan (2013) are to explore the post-foreclosure experience of U.S. households. They determined how a foreclosure affects, if at all, a household's consumption, composition, and propensity to move. This topic is relatively under-examined. Most existing research regarding this topic deals mainly with the causes and preventions to foreclosures, rather than the effects they have on households. Since the most recent financial crisis is so recent, data required to answer some of these questions is limited. However, through isolating certain characteristics of U.S. households before and after foreclosure, Molloy and Shan (2013) are able to derive several interesting conclusions.

The data Molloy and Shan (2013) relied on was an analysis of credit reports from the FRBNY/Equifax Consumer Credit Panel. This report comprised a random sample of 5 percent of U.S. individuals with credit files, including their household members. This data set accounted for roughly 15 percent of the adult population, or approximately 37 million individuals. The data tracks these individuals and their activity on a quarterly basis from 1999 to the present.

In order to determine how much of the activity within this sample can be attributed to the effects of foreclosure on individuals, Molloy and Shan created a comparison group using data from the year prior to a foreclosure start. This group is composed of individuals that have similar characteristics (age, credit score, mortgage balance, etc.), but did not experience a foreclosure on their home. Through this comparison they were able to better understand if foreclosure, or possibly other external factors, affects the way the sample population behaves. Their research focused on answering a few main questions regarding the behavior of post-foreclosure households.

One aspect of the Molloy and Shan (2013) research is that it dealt with a household's propensity to move, and whether or not foreclosure on their home made them more likely to move. In order to answer this question, they tracked a sample group of households who all experienced foreclosure starting in the same year. Then, they tracked these households and compared them to the comparison group over a four-year period. The beginning of this period was the year prior to foreclosure and continued all the way to three years after foreclosure. Using this data, they were able to track any differences between the two groups to better understand how foreclosures can affect a household's desire to move and at what point during the foreclosure process this is most evident.

Another topic Molloy and Shan (2013) addressed was, if the household decided to migrate, what were these post-foreclosure migration patterns. In order to analyze this data, they used an individual's address as the key variable in the data. Additionally, they also used detailed geographic identifiers provided by the FRBY/ Equifax Consumer Credit Panel. They compared and contrasted the sample group to the comparison group in terms of migration distance. In order to create the most accurate sampling, they removed non-movers from the comparison group in order to isolate the migrating individuals only. Using this information, they were able to determine the migration distance between households, as well as any significant changes in neighborhood demographics.

The results of Molloy and Shan (2013) showed that foreclosure did in fact cause a slight change in lifestyle compared to the non-foreclosure group, but not as drastic as some may think. To start, the data for a household's propensity to move showed that 50 percent of foreclosed individuals move within the first three years of the foreclosure process. In contrast, only about 25 percent of non-foreclosed individuals in the sample moved. While the evidence suggests that post-foreclosed individuals are more likely to move, they do not usually end up living in worse conditions than their comparison group.

One aspect that remains largely the same for post-foreclosed individuals is household size. Information on household size gathered by reports from the FRBNY/Equifax Consumer Credit Panel concluded that post-foreclosed individuals did not experience a decline in size compared to the control group. Although the size of the household is not affected, there were a few other factors that highlight the efforts of going through foreclosure.

Access to credit is much more difficult for post-foreclosed individuals. This would make sense, but the lack of credit also leads to other unfavorable outcomes for the group. Mortgages were hard to come by for post-foreclosed borrowers as only 6 percent had one just two years after their foreclosure. As a result of the lack of credit and mortgages, people who experienced a foreclosure were much more likely to move into multi-family housing rather than single-family. About 22 percent of foreclosed borrowers switched from single-family to multi-family housing from 2006 to 2008. In contrast, it was only 3 percent of people in the comparison group during that time.

Post-foreclosure is not a topic that has been heavily studied after the housing crisis, but Molloy and Shan (2013) highlight some of the main tangible effects that the foreclosure process has on an individual. For example, access to credit is something that is greatly affected for those who have experienced foreclosure. Mortgages are much harder to come by. Single-family housing becomes much more difficult. All of these different hoops to jump through, but ultimately post-foreclosed individuals are able to consume as much and live in the same size houses as the comparison group, they just do it by different means instead of getting a mortgage, people rent. Instead of downsizing housing, post-foreclosed individuals move in with different people and keep the same quality of living. Ultimately, foreclosure does have a slight negative effect on a person's ability to find housing and be financial stable, but at the end both groups have strong chances of climbing out of whatever struggle they are in with smart planning.

Molloy and Shan (2013) has a few similarities with the theories and ideas taught in Mian and Sufi (2014). The main connection is when Mian and Sufi (2014) talk about marginal borrowers, those who probably would not be able to get a mortgage without an expansion of credit. In Molloy and Shan (2013), the post-foreclosed individuals are the marginal borrowers because of their difficulty in obtaining a mortgage. In turn, many of them were forced into renting and multi-family housing because of a lack of credit.

Molloy and Shan (2013) did an excellent job in going into great detail about the post-foreclosure experience. However, they could have possibly established better context for the reader beforehand.

One suggestion would be to be able to add another comparison group to make three groups in total. That way, one could isolate some of the variables that go into organizing the groups to allow for a more precise comparison. Seeing how post-foreclosed individuals responded to the housing crisis would have been more educational had there been two different types of comparison groups.

Molloy and Shan (2013) left the door open for more research on the post-foreclosure process. While most research was done on the immediate effects of foreclosure (1–2 years.), there can be valuable insight on the long-term effects of foreclosure. For example, one could see the likelihood of foreclosing again having experienced one, or the levels of credit different people have at different times of the post-foreclosure process.

## Multiple Choice Questions

1. According to Molloy and Shan (2013), which of the following is true regarding migration patterns of post-foreclosure households two years after they have received a foreclosure start?

    (a) Migration begins to increase at a higher rate than in the previous two years

    (b) Migration remains at the same rate than in the previous two years

    **(c) Significantly less migration is seen than in the previous two years**

**Explanation:** A foreclosure start is the moment in time in which a bank begins the total foreclosure process on a homeowner's property. The data our author's gathered showed that a foreclosure start significantly increases the probability that a homeowner will move. After two years, the number of households choosing to migrate tapers off in comparison to the jump in years one and two. Not only that, but about half of all homeowners that were foreclosed on do not move at all. This data suggest that the foreclosure process, for many homes, is frequently never completed. This situation is most common in judicial states, where the foreclosure process must go through the courts, or in areas with rapid house appreciation, where loans be refinanced more easily.

2. According to Molloy and Shan (2013), which of the following is true regarding housing consumption of post-foreclosure borrowers?

   (a) Due to a reduction in access to credit, borrowers see a significant drop-off in household consumption
   
   **(b) While there are certain adverse outcomes, the decrease in consumption of post-foreclosure borrowers, on average, is only minor**
   
   (c) Household consumption dropped more in judicial states where courts made it more difficult to finish the foreclosure process in a timely manner
   
   (d) (a) and (c)

**Explanation:** Contrary to popular belief, household consumption dropped only slightly in post-foreclosure borrowers across the country. There are a number of reasons or scenarios that would support these findings. The main reason the author's cited for this surprising result is that households tend to save less in these times while spending the same regarding household consumption. Through this scenario, borrowers' consumption appears to remain the same. However, the borrower in reality is saving much less income and is even more vulnerable to further financial downturn. This conclusion would suggest that the demand for housing consumption would be very inelastic.

3. According to Molloy and Shan (2013), which of the following is true regarding post-foreclosed individuals?

   I. They are more likely to move in with friends or family member following a foreclosure
   
   II. They tend to switch to mortgage-free housing
   
   III. They have lower quality housing compared to non-foreclosed individuals
   
   (a) I only
   
   (b) I and III

**(c) I and II**
(d) II only

**Explanation:** Foreclosure affected people in a number of ways, but surprisingly it did not have any effect on housing quality compared to those who did not foreclose. At first, it seems like they would move into lower quality housing, but instead they just made smarter, less risky living arrangements like apartments and moving in with friends or family. Thus, a higher percentage of them switched to mortgage free housing in the immediate years after a foreclosure. By doing this, they are able to ease the financial responsibility of a mortgage and allocate resources elsewhere.

## References

Mian, A. and A. Sufi (2014), *House of Debt*, USA: The University of Chicago Press.
Molloy R. and H. Shan (2013), "The Post-foreclosure Experience of U.S. Households", *Real Estate Economics* 41, 225–254.

# Chapter 15

# Foreclosure Externalities

*In collaboration with* Josh Feldman and T. J. Pyzyk

It is obvious that foreclosures have a destructive effect on the households which have to default on their loans and lose their homes. This destruction is not isolated, though, and often creates spillover effects that affect the communities around them. These spillover effects are called negative externalities, and understanding how these externalities play a part in the exacerbation of economic events is key to understanding the big picture of how the subprime mortgage crisis affected the economy as a whole.

The question at hand is if an area with a high concentration of subprime mortgages has an effect on the probability of default in its surrounding areas. The motivation for investigating this question is the housing bubble in the United States. In order to make sense of the economic shock the housing market underwent, Agarwal *et al.* (2012) investigated how the concentration of risky mortgages affected the default rates in a specific area. In "Thy Neighbor's Mortgage: Does Living in a Subprime Neighborhood Affect One's Probability of Default?," they try to prove that subprime mortgage concentration in a certain area is unrelated to the default risks that area faces. Instead, the negative effects of aggressive mortgage products do have an impact on other borrowers within the same area, specifically, hybrid adjustable rate mortgages (ARMs) and loans that were given when low or no documentation was provided. Overall, the goal of Agarwal *et al.* (2012) was to illustrate how during the years leading up to the Great Recession, aggressive mortgage products played a more significant role impacting the probability of default for other borrowers than subprime mortgages did.

In order to prove the claims made above, Agarwal *et al.* (2012) provided data collected from several different agencies, along with examples to show the effects of different mortgages in certain areas. The data focus on Maricopa County in Arizona, where data on 461,729 mortgages originated between the years 2000 and 2007 is used as a reference. The majority of the data were collected from the asset-backed securities data series within the Loan Performance Corporation, or LPC. From 2000 to 2007 we see a dramatic increase in the total number of mortgages generated in Phoenix, from 10,653 to 145,333 from 2000 to 2005, of which 67.3 percent were classified as subprime, while 32.4 percent were classified as Alt-A mortgages. During this time period the value of houses also sky rocketed, the Case Schiller Home Price Index shows a year over year price change in Phoenix from 100.00 at the beginning of 2000 to 227.42 by the middle of 2006. This growth rate was much faster than the rate at which housing prices were changing throughout the country. As the increase in total mortgages originated from 2000 to 2007 we see a decrease in the documentation being provided in order to receive a mortgage. In 2000, 75 percent of mortgages were given after the borrower provided full documentation; in 2006 that number drastically drops to a mere 41 percent. Agarwal *et al.* (2012) observed the decrease in documentation being provided by borrowers as well as the increase in ARMs going from 46 percent in 2000 to 65 percent in 2004 as a proportion of all mortgages originated. Essentially, over the time period of 2000–2007 in Phoenix, risky mortgages became far more prevalent.

After pointing out the change in mortgage practices that the data shows in the early 2000's, Agarwal *et al.* (2012) wanted to see the impact these behaviors had on defaults. During the interval of 2000–2005 the average monthly default rate was consistently less than 1 percent, but this percentage more than doubled in the year 2006 when it was 2.34 percent. It is clear that something caused this spike in default rates from year to year. When looking at subprime, Alt-A, and low/no documentation mortgage concentration in search of an explanation, they saw subprime mortgage concentration peaked in 2005 at 12 percent from a 4.5 percent in 2000; on the other hand, over this same period from 2000 to 2005 the concentration of Alt-A mortgages increased by 600 percent and low/no documentation loans by an even more staggering margin of 800 percent.

When analyzing the correlation between different types of mortgages concentration and default risk, Agarwal *et al.* (2012) made assumptions about the way in which people behave. The option-pricing model held all factors constant and directly analyzed the relationship between housing value and mortgage defaults and was founded on the idea that borrowers default when the property value becomes less than the mortgage value. Also, they assumed that the situation described above is the only instance where a borrower will default on his or her mortgage. It is also important to address that they expected homeowners to observe and respond to the noisy private signals that were relevant to their property. Noisy signals came in two forms, high signals and low signals. High signals implied that the property market is appreciating; on the contrary, low signals suggested that the property market is decreasing. An example of a noisy signal is how long properties are available on the market, a long time would be a low signal, and a short time would be a high signal. In some situations, the homeowner defaults and the low noisy signal causes other homes to depreciate in value, resulting in those homes also defaulting. These situations are referred to as foreclosure cascades. This is basically a domino effect that begins with one foreclosure and causes all property values to decrease one by one thus being less than their respective mortgages and resulting in a default. A foreclosure cascade is much more likely to happen in an area where the homeowners are highly levered because a small decrease in their property value can cause it to fall below the value of their large mortgage. The model Agarwal *et al.* (2012) used focuses on individual mortgages, and using two functions, the cumulative density function, and the probability density function. In order to determine the hazard function for each mortgage, they used risk factors such as the borrowers risk characteristics, what type of loan it was, mortgage concentration measures that were ZIP code specific, changes in house prices, and foreclosures in nearby areas.

The results of Agarwal *et al.* (2012) were that the credit score of the borrower and default risk are inversely related, meaning that as credit scores increase default risk decreases. In addition, loan-to-value (LTV) ratios are positively correlated with default risk, meaning that higher levered loans have a higher risk of default. Subprime loans were found to default 1.3 more times than prime loans. Borrowers who provided low documentation defaulted 1.8 more times than full documentation loans; no documentation loans defaulted even more frequently at 2.4 times more than full documentation loans. Fixed-rate mortgages also showed a default rate half of that of hybrid ARMs. Subprime mortgages appeared negatively correlated with borrower risk. Default risk decreased as the concentration of subprime mortgages increased in a given area. ARMs and no/low documentation mortgages were positively correlated with default rates. For each additional 1 percent increase of hybrid ARMS in an area, the default risk increased by 2.4 percent. The same 1 percent increase of no/low documentation mortgages in an area resulted in a 10 percent increase in default rates. Finally, for every 1 percent increase in foreclosures in a specific ZIP code the default rate increased by 2.9 percent.

In conclusion, Agarwal *et al.* (2012) found an interesting mix of results, some of which were expected and some were unexpected. When looking at the relationship between default and subprime mortgages on the local level of Phoenix, Arizona, they found that subprime mortgages are not evenly spread throughout cities, instead they are highly concentrated in low-income areas. They expected this result considering low-income individuals are more likely to not qualify for a prime mortgage and have to opt for a subprime mortgage. Also as expected, they found that riskier borrower and loan characteristics, like high LTV ratios, low credit scores, and alternative loan structures, result in a higher probability of default. They also concluded that if there is a high rate of foreclosure in an area, borrowers in that area are more likely to default.

Unexpectedly, Agarwal *et al.* (2012) did not find that concentrations of subprime lending resulted in a higher risk of defaults in the area. From this finding, they conclude that lending to subprime borrowers in itself does not increase the risk of default, but subprime lending creates a greater availability of credit, resulting in house prices being driven up. They also found that more aggressive and riskier mortgage products increased the probability of borrower default. In other words, the increase in subprime lending drove housing prices up due to the availability of credit, then rising house prices would encourage people to take on riskier types of mortgage products, which continued to push housing prices up, continuing in a vicious cycle, ultimately resulting in the bubble.

This conclusion is very much in line with Mian and Sufi (2014). Mian and Sufi (2014) analyze the housing crisis from a multitude of economic points of view but ultimately concluded that the housing bubble and resulting crisis was the result of an increase in the availability of consumer credit. Agarwal *et al.* (2012) findings seem to coincide and back Mian and Sufi (2014). Both reject the fundamentalist and animal spirits views of the economic crisis and find an increased supply of credit is to blame.

While Agarwal *et al.* (2012) do make some very good points and back them up with good research, the paper is not without its weaknesses. The paper focuses completely on Phoenix, AZ as a market. They would have created a stronger case if they had tried to examine other markets and see if their findings held. Furthermore, they picked one of the markets most heavily affected by the economic crisis. It would be interesting to see how their findings hold in a less volatile market. They also found that ARMs were negatively correlated with default risk; however, it would be interesting to see a historical study on this finding. Interest rates could have been favorable for borrowers at the time of the crisis, which would help decrease the rate of default.

In the future, it would be interesting for Agarwal *et al.* (2012) to do research on a wider scale and look at more cities from around the country. Real estate markets vary greatly from city to city and regionally in the United States. It would be interesting to see if they would have similar findings in various regions of the U.S. Furthermore, considering they found subprime loans are concentrated near the central business districts of cities, it would be interesting to see similar research performed on a non-urban area. There are many rural lower-income areas that would be interesting to see juxtaposed to their findings on urban areas.

## Multiple Choice Questions

1. According to Agarwal *et al.* (2012), which aspects of a mortgage were found to indicate a riskier mortgage?
   (a) Low Borrower Credit Quality
   (b) High LTV Ratios
   (c) Classification as Subprime or Alt-A
   **(d) All of the above**

**Explanation:** As expected, Agarwal *et al.* (2012) found borrower credit quality, LTV ratios, and classification as subprime or Alt-A to be indicators of a higher risk mortgage. The authors used Fair Isaac Corporation (FICO) scores to indicate borrower credit quality and found higher FICO scores to be correlated with lower mortgage quality. This makes sense and is expected because someone who has had good credit and paid their bills in the past is likely to make payments in the future. Higher LTV ratios or LTV ratios also makes sense and are expected as they generally indicate larger mortgages and borrowers that have less available funds to buy a house. Also, for houses with a high LTV, it takes less of a loss for the house to be "underwater" which incentivizes default. Classification as subprime or Alt-A also makes sense because these types of mortgages usually have higher interest rates, LTVs, or borrowers were poorer credit histories.

2. According to Agarwal *et al.* (2012), what correlation did ARMs have with higher default risks?
   **(a) Negative and significant**
   (b) Positive and significant

(c)  Negative and insignificant

(d)  Positive and insignificant

**Explanation:** Many people in the media pointed the blame at and spent a lot of time discussing ARMs. At face value, it might make sense to assume a mortgage that puts interest rate risk on the side of the borrower would increase default risk; however, the authors found ARMs to have a significantly lower default rate than FRMs or fixed rate mortgages. This may be because ARMs generally have a lower interest rate. There also could have been lower interest rates surrounding the mortgage crisis.

3.  According to Agarwal *et al.* (2012), what correlation did mortgage documentation have with default risk?

   **(a)  Low-documentation was correlated with higher default risk**

   (b)  High-documentation was correlated with higher default risk

   (c)  Documentation was not correlated with default risk

   (d)  Low-documentation was correlated with lower default risk

**Explanation:** Agarwal *et al.* (2012) found that borrowers that originated loans with either low or no documentation were found to be 1.8–2.4 times more likely to default than borrowers that provide documentation of their income and assets. They also found that in 2000, 75 percent of borrowers provided full documentation, but by 2006 only 41 percent of borrowers were providing full documentation of assets and income, 55 percent were providing low documentation, and 3 percent were providing no documentation. These findings make sense as less information about the financial status of the borrower should be associated with higher default risk.

## References

Agarwal, S., B. W. Ambrose, S. Chomsisengphet and A. B. Sanders (2012), "Thy Neighbor's Mortgage: Does Living in a Subprime Neighborhood Affect One's Probability of Default?", *Real Estate Economics* 40, 1–22.

Mian, A. and A. Sufi (2014), *House of Debt*, USA: The University of Chicago Press.

# Part III
# Government Intervention

# Chapter 16

# The Role of the Affordable Housing Goals

*In collaboration with* Louis Pelletier
and Tyler Finn

While beliefs differ as to what caused the subprime crisis, one popular theory is that the Affordable Housing Goals (AHG) instituted by the Clinton administration increased the prevalence of subprime lending by the government sponsored enterprises (GSEs), making things much worse when the bubble ultimately popped. To understand some of the circumstances in relation to the housing bubble, it is important to look at the role of GSEs. The first GSE was Fannie Mae. Fannie Mae and later Freddie Mac were created to increase liquidity within the credit market, and to also help maintain the secondary mortgage market. Originally, Fannie Mae purchased only Federal Housing Administration (FHA) insured mortgages, but eventually it began to purchase other classes of mortgages.

Essentially the goal of the GSEs was to alleviate mortgage originator's risk and perpetuate additional lending to promote housing. The increase in homeownership during this time was in direct fulfillment of the Clinton administration's priority of increasing homeownership. In order to achieve this, in 1995 the administration unveiled their AHG. There were three of them, with each having different criteria for a property to qualify. The first goal was the Low to Moderate Income Goal, the second goal was the Special Affordable Goal, and the third was the Underserved Areas Goal (UAG).

Bolotnyy (2014) took up the question of whether these goals caused the GSEs to purchase more subprime loans than they otherwise would have. Specifically, Bolotnyy looked at how much of an effect the UAG had on loan purchases by GSEs, and uses these results to judge whether or not the other goals were effective as well. For a residence to qualify for the UAG, this residence had to be part of a census tract whose median income is less than 90 percent of the median for an area family, or less than 120 percent of the area median and a minimum minority population of 30 percent.

In order to examine this effect, Bolotnyy (2014) took data at the census tract level from Housing and Urban Development (HUD) for single-family loans that the GSEs had purchased from 1993 to 2006. Relative to the sources used by other studies he reviewed, Bolotnyy believed that this data would help him achieve better results because it accounts for loans the GSEs purchased a year after origination somewhere else ("Seasoned") and loans they did not buy straight from the originator. He also used a different time period (1993–1995) for his control years than Bhutta (2014), who used 1994–1996. Because Bolotnyy believed Bhutta's choice of time period would skew the results, he chose a different period. From there, he estimated the effect of the UAG goal for two different time periods and two different types of tracts: a general effect from 1996 to 2002, and the effect on homes that were not in tracts targeted by the goals during the 2001–2002 time frame, but had become targeted by 2005–2006.

When structuring his model for the 1996–2002 time period, Bolotnyy first made an important assumption to simplify his analysis: because the data did not include how many residences were being bought with each mortgage, he assumed that a single-family loan was going toward the purchase of one home. Bolotnyy was trying to find whether there was a significant difference in purchasing activity between tracts in targeted areas, and tracts in areas that were not targeted. Tracts are differentiated by their TM ratio, or the ratio of tract income to metropolitan statistical area income. Bolotnyy compared the tracts that were just below and at the threshold of being eligible for the UAG with tracts that were just above the threshold; he used the 90 percent income rule of the UAG as the threshold for his comparison, and ran the analysis at three different levels of significance: 0.02, 0.05 and 0.10, respectively. 0.9 was chosen because tracts with a ratio at or below 0.8 would also be eligible for other programs, so he did not want to capture the effects of unrelated policies. The intuition here is that if the housing goals contributed to the subprime crisis, one would see higher purchasing activity in tracts with a ratio below 0.9 than tracts with a ratio at or above 0.9.

The second model is where Bolotnyy analyzed the UAG effect on GSE activity in tracts that were not targeted by the goals in 2001–2002, but had become targeted by 2005–2006. He did this to account for the 2000 census data that had become the basis for tracking goals instead of the 1990 data used for the earlier period. These regressions were run at the same three significance levels. The intuition would seem to be that if one assumed the goals had contributed to GSE purchasing activity, there would be a lot of purchases in tracts that switched to being targeted.

After running his analyses, Bolotnyy found some interesting results. During the analysis of 1996–2002, the data showed that the amount of loans purchased with a TM ratio just below the 0.9 threshold was very close to the amount of loans purchased that were just above the threshold: 1,055 vs. 1,016, respectively. This difference is not statistically important. Furthermore, at the 0.02 level of significance, there were only about 1.1 percent more loans from targeted tracts than tracts that were not targeted — another finding that is not statistically significant. Finally, there was an overall UAG effect of 2.7 percent; this is not a statistically significant difference from zero according to Bolotnyy (2014), and as a result he concluded that the UAG had a negligible effect at best on GSE purchasing behavior during this time.

The second analysis also produced interesting, counterintuitive results. The most significant result of this analysis is that during the

2005–2006 period, significantly more loans were purchased in tracts that had not switched to being targeted, with the difference deemed statistically important by Bolotnyy (2014). The purchases for each tract per year were 87.40 for tracts that switched and 114.99 for ones that maintained their status. If anything, the GSEs were actually purchasing better quality loans, not the poor quality ones it was generally assumed they'd been buying. Bolotnyy reached the conclusion that on average, the UAG effect for tracts whose status switched was about 2.9 percent. He did not believe that his findings for either scenario were statistically significant, and thus concludes that the goals did not play an important role in the purchasing activity of the GSEs during this time period either.

Bolotnyy's main goal of the paper was to discover if the AHGs led to an increase in risky mortgage purchases by the Government-Sponsored Enterprises. Effectively, he tried to see if the AHGs were the cause of the subprime mortgage crisis that started in the mid-2000s, and was a main reason for one of the U.S.' biggest financial crises. After testing the effect of the UAG on mortgage purchasing activity, Bolotnyy concluded that the AHGs did not play a factor in the purchasing behavior of the GSEs, which goes directly against the conventional wisdom of the topic.

There were many interesting connections between Bolotnyy (2014) and the Mian and Sufi (2014) book, *House of Debt*. The most relevant one is that both works reach conclusions that refute conventional wisdom upon actual analysis of the data. A particular example of this is a survey of small business owners run during 2007 and 2009 in Mian and Sufi (2014). The conventional wisdom about small business is that they are especially dependent upon bank credit for survival; as a result, during the Great Recession they would likely cite banking issues as one of their biggest worries. However, this was not the case. When asked about their biggest concern, the portion that chose "financing and interest rates," was extremely low; this number was always at or below 5 percent, and even decreased between 2007 and 2009. This is very similar to the fact that the AHGs had little actual effect on the GSE activity, which refutes much of the conventional wisdom of the subprime crisis.

One weakness in Bolotnyy (2014) is that he only tests the effect of a single housing goal. He gives no reason as to why he chose to test the UAG compared to the other two goals. A more complete analysis would have been testing each goal and then coming up with a conclusion based on that. If he decided to test for only one goal, it may have made more sense to test the effect of the Low and Moderate-Income Goal. This goal is more related to risky lending because low-income individuals were the ones engaging in the riskiest loans. This analysis would more likely show if there was an effect of the AHGs on the GSE purchasing behavior compared to the UAG.

## Multiple Choice Questions

1. According to Bolotnyy (2014), what were some of the limitations in similar papers regarding the effect of the AHGs?

    (a) Analyses unable to take GSE Purchases of Seasoned Mortgages

    (b) Analyses unable to take GSE purchases of mortgages not sold directly to the GSE

    (c) Use of wrong years as control years that bias the results

    **(d) All of the above**

**Explanation:** Bolotnyy (2014) mentioned existing literature on the GSEs and the mortgage crisis. He attempts to improve the analysis by past experts. Bolotnyy (2014) explains some of his peers' biggest limitations in their papers were using the wrong years as control years. One paper by Bhutta (2014) used 1994–1996 as pre-UAG control years. This is a limit because Bolotnyy notes that preliminary goals were set into place as early as 1993. Thus, Bhutta's (2014) results are likely biased downward. Bolotnyy (2014) used 1993–1994 as control years rather than the years mentioned earlier. The overall biggest limitation is related to data. HMDA data was used in past literature, and this database did not include purchases of seasoned mortgages or mortgages that were not sold directly to the GSE. Bolotnyy (2014) overcame this limitation by using data through HUD's GSE Public Use Database (this info is available in this database).

2. According to Bolotnyy (2014), what was the effect of the AHGs, specifically the UAG, on the GSE's purchasing of mortgages?

    (a) It caused the GSE's to purchase to many mortgages, which sparked the Financial Crisis

    **(b) The AHGs were not drivers of the subprime market and the financial crisis**

    (c) It caused the GSE's to purchase too few mortgages, which had a relatively high effect in perpetuating the Financial Crisis

    (d) Bolotnyy was unable to make a conclusion due to the insufficient data

**Explanation:** Bolotnyy (2014) found that the GSE purchases of mortgages are not more concentrated in the targeted goal areas. This means that the GSE was purchasing mortgages because they still believed that it would be profitable, and were not doing it based off of Clinton's Housing Goals. The effect of the Housing Goals was extremely minimal in relation to GSE purchases in poor/underserved areas. High-risk borrowers were responsible for the financial crisis, and Bolotnyy believes that the Housing Goals were not responsible for increasing the number of these high-risk borrowers.

3. Valentin Bolotnyy used what AHG(s) to test the effect on the GSE mortgage purchases?

    **(a) Underserved Areas Goal (UAG)**

    (b) Low and Moderate-Income Goal (LMG)

    (c) Special Affordable Goals (SAG)

    (d) All three of them

**Explanation:** Bolotnyy (2014) tested only the effect of the first goal, the UAG. He did this because he believed the results from his analysis of the UAG could be a measure for the effectiveness of all the goals. It also seems that he examined this goal in particular because the other literature he reviewed used this goal, and he wanted to make a direct comparison between his results and theirs.

# References

Bolotnyy, V. (2014), "The Government-Sponsored Enterprises and the Mortgage Crisis: The Role of the Affordable Housing Goals", *Real Estate Economics* 42, 724–755.

Bhutta, N. (2014), "GSE Activity and Mortgage Supply in Lower-Income and Minority Neighborhoods: The Effect of the Affordable Housing Goals", *Journal of Real Estate Finance and Ecomomics* 45, 238–261.

Mian, A. and A. Sufi (2014), *House of Debt*, USA: The University of Chicago Press.

# Chapter 17

# The Fed's MBS Mortgage Program

*In collaboration with* Jack Ferguson
and Rebecca Jin

During the years of 1999–2006, subprime lending was very popular and it made it very easy for many Americans to attain a home. This subprime lending seemed like a prosperous idea to many people until it proved to be detrimental to the U.S. economy. For example, an individual with inadequate savings and a less than ideal credit score was able to take out a mortgage that often contained a high-interest rate to reflect the risk involved. A commercial investor could then come along and purchase mortgage-backed securities (MBSs), which were a pool of mortgages grouped into one security. These investors profited off of the premium and interest paid by the subprime individuals, so the investments were profitable as long as house prices continued to rise and payments could be made. Once housing prices began to plummet, this subprime individual's home could worth less than the amount they owed on their mortgage. The individual may then have to default on their mortgage, ultimately affecting the investor that purchased the subprime mortgage through an MBS. Cases such as this were common all over the country leading up to the economic recession, and it was only a matter of time before the Federal Reserve would be forced to step in and intervene in the economy.

The Federal Reserve announced a MBS purchase program on November 25, 2008. The Federal Reserve purchased up to $500 billion in MBS backed by Fannie Mae and Freddie Mac, also known as government sponsored enterprises (GSEs). Hancock and Passmore (2011) aim to break down the three channels in which the program affected mortgage rates. These three channels include improved market functioning in primary and secondary mortgage markets, clear government backing of Fannie Mae and Freddie Mac, and the anticipation of portfolio rebalancing effects. Hancock and Passmore (2011) made it their goal to explain how clearer government backing and improved market functioning could reduce abnormal market pricing in primary and secondary mortgage markets. They also investigate the rebalancing effect and how under certain conditions it influenced mortgage rates. They use empirical models to measure the effects of each channel, and they hypothesized that the announcement of the MBS program would result in lower mortgage rates by 100 basis points for purchasing homes.

Hancock and Passmore (2011) utilized data from various sources to support their hypothesis. They collected MBS purchase and issuance data from eMBS.com. They also obtained data on variables that would affect MBS prices and mortgage rates from Bloomberg. These variables included prepayment risk, basis risk, and rollover risk. To chart the changes in mortgage rates over time, they acquired mortgage rate information from Freddie Mac. Having this data allowed them to analyze how certain variables affected MBS yields and mortgage rates, graph the changes in mortgage rates, and helped them conclude the purchase program's effect of lowering mortgage rates.

When homeowners buy a house, they can finance the house with a mortgage. The mortgage provider then sets a rate at which the homeowner will pay back the mortgage. To set the price, the provider has to consider risks that he or she may incur, such as if the homeowner prepays the mortgage. The provider eventually collects and sells these mortgages to GSEs, Fannie Mae or Freddie

Mac, and helps raise the supply of credit available to those who are looking to purchase a house. Fannie Mae and Freddie Mac purchase such mortgages and pack them together to create MBSs, insuring them so that in the case of mortgage defaults, the principal and interest of these mortgages still gets paid to investors (Stroebel and Taylor, 2012).

The GSEs, Fannie Mae and Freddie Mac, were granted conservatorship by the Federal Housing Finance Agency (FHFA) on September 7, 2008. To support the FHFA's act, the United States Department of Treasury took three steps. First, the Treasury established Preferred Stock Purchase Agreements to help each company retain positive net worth. Second, the Treasury created a secure lending credit facility that would help provide short-term loans to GSEs if needed, thus providing a temporary liquidity backstop. Third, the Treasury would purchase GSE MBS on a temporary basis to maintain mortgage credit availability (Jickling, 2008). The U.S. government took such steps to demonstrate support for Fannie Mae and Freddie Mac.

Once mortgages get packed into securities, buyers such as depository institutions, foreign buyers, and GSEs can purchase these securities and add them to their portfolios. However, a recession hit around December 2007. Many buyers had limited funds and decreased confidence to purchase more MBSs, thus demand for Fannie Mae and Freddie Mac MBS fell.

To relieve the financial crisis and improve mortgage rates, the Federal Reserve utilized an MBS purchase program. This was a part of the Federal Reserve's plan to "ease credit" and reduce high credit spreads. The objective of the purchase program was to decrease mortgage rates through three channels: improve market functioning in the primary and secondary mortgage markets, demonstrate apparent government support for Fannie Mae and Freddie Mac, and give a clearer direction of the effects of investors rebalancing their portfolios. The Federal Reserve believed that improving market functioning and providing clearer government backing would help decrease fluctuations in MBS pricing in the primary and secondary mortgage markets.

Although there was a delay between the announcement and implementation of the purchase program, after the program was announced, mortgage market analysts commended the government's decision. Analysts saw this as a sign of the government clearly supporting the mortgage market. Market participants also commended this decision, which they believed would help resolve ambiguity in the government's support for the mortgage market, as well as problems with illiquidity and price discovery.

The Federal Reserve's MBS purchase program spanned through five distinct time periods:

1. July 2000–March 2004: The "pre-subprime" mortgage period.
2. April 2004–July 2007: The "subprime dominance" period.
3. August 2007–November 2008: The financial crisis.
4. November 2008–March 2010: The Federal Reserve's intervention in the MBS market.
5. April 2010–August 2010: Post-Fed intervention.

Throughout these five periods, Hancock and Passmore (2011) measured the MBS swap-spread and mortgage rate-MBS spread throughout the purchase program and created time series regressions to determine the fluctuation of mortgage rates. Analyzing these two spreads allowed them to study how the banks in the secondary market hedged their MBS portfolios against risks such as interest rate, funding, illiquidity, and the mark-ups the banks made to offset costs from such risks that affected mortgage rate pricing. Such mark-ups determined the fluctuations in mortgage rates, and analyzing these rates enabled them to study the change in mortgage rates before, during, and after the purchase program.

First, Hancock and Passmore (2011) measured the MBS yield during the "pre-subprime" mortgage period, while mortgage rates were still at "normal" levels. MBS yields were charted as a linear function of the long-term swap rate, the short-term swap-to-Treasury spread, prepayment rates, and rollover risks. According to Stroebel and Taylor (2012), the swap rate is the rate that the homeowner pays so that they can pay a variable interest rate instead of a fixed interest rate on their mortgage. Each of these determinants represented a type of risk that the MBS holder took when setting prices for their MBS. The MBS holder priced accordingly to minimize losses, in preparation for a crisis such as the Great Recession. The data demonstrated that long swap rates, prepayment risks, and rollover risks had significant effects on MBS yields.

Long swap rates were positively correlated with MBS yields, with a coefficient of 1.06 and a high, significant $t$-value of 76.61. Such a correlation indicated that market participants price their MBS accordingly with long swap rates, such that when long swap rates increased by 1 percent, market participants would increase their MBS yields 106 basis points (or 1.06 percent). Prepayment risks and rollover risks were also positively correlated with MBS yields, with coefficients of 25 basis points and 0.82 basis points and significant $t$-values of 11.56 and 12.92, respectively. With positive coefficients, each of these determinants positively contributed and increased MBS yields. When market participants perceived prepayment risks and rollover risks to be high, they priced their MBS higher to offset such risks.

Next, Hancock and Passmore modeled mortgage rates against the MBS yield and the home price index. The mortgage rate was considered to be a mark-up above MBS yields to account for possible risks and cost. After taking weekly data between July 2000 and March 2004 (during the "pre-subprime" mortgage period), Hancock and Passmore found that MBS yields were positively correlated with mortgage rates, with a large $t$-value of 32.41. Thus, MBS yield was a significant determinant of mortgage rates. Home price indices were also recorded weekly in that same period of time and found to be negatively correlated with mortgage rates, consistent with the theory that costs associated with mortgages will decrease as house prices increase. They found that as the home price index increased by 1 percent, mortgage rates would decrease by 0.0054 percent.

Then, Hancock and Passmore (2011) continued their investigation by measuring mortgage rates as a mark-up over the MBS yield, during the purchase program, to make a comparison with market data from that before the financial crisis occurred, and determine whether or not the purchase program was effective in reducing mortgage rates. The market data showed that MBS pricing had minimal fluctuation up until mid-2005 (around the time of the "subprime dominance" period). During the financial crisis, MBS yields also had little fluctuation, and actual yields were only 16 basis points less than the predicted MBS yields. As the purchase program progressed, MBS yields fluctuated less and less due to market participants gaining confidence in the Federal Reserve's objective to improve the mortgage market.

Finally, Hancock and Passmore (2011) measured the effects of the mortgage purchase program by calculating the changes in abnormal mortgage pricing, abnormal MBS pricing, compensation to protect against interest rate risks, compensation to protect against prepayment risks, and primary mortgage costs. The mortgage rate was set as a function of the MBS yield and primary mortgage costs, which then allowed the authors to set the change in mortgage rate as a function of the changes in abnormal mortgage pricing, abnormal MBS pricing, interest rate hedging costs, volatility hedging costs, and primary mortgage market costs. By measuring the effects in changes in abnormal market pricing in the mortgage and MBS markets, they demonstrated improved market functioning and clearer government backing. Changes in interest rate hedging costs and volatility hedging costs provide evidence of investor demand for MBS, and the Federal Reserve's MBS purchase program was able to lower mortgage rates, and in turn raise demand for portfolio rebalancing in favor of mortgages.

Upon charting all the data, Hancock and Passmore (2011) were able to conclude that mortgage rates decreased with the help of the Federal Reserve's MBS purchase program. With the announcement of the purchase program, mortgage rates declined by 82 basis points. Such an announcement provided clarity of government support for the program, and as a result, there was a decline in abnormal mortgage pricing, MBS pricing, and interest costs, all of which indicate less investment risk. Overall, during the federal intervention period, mortgage rates fell by 2 basis points and then rose 9 basis points. By May 27, 2009, around the middle of the Federal Reserve's intervention, markets were in complete understanding of the purchase program objectives, and the mortgage market was set on a stabilizing path, despite a slight growth in mortgage rates. By the end of the program, mortgage rates had declined by 64 basis points. Altogether, from the beginning of the program when the Federal Reserve announced their MBS purchase program, until a post-Federal Reserve intervention period, mortgage rates fell by a total of 139 basis points.

Hancock and Passmore (2011) charted mortgage rate fluctuations and showed that the Federal Reserve MBS purchase program helped decrease mortgage rates and increase demand for MBS. Their data supported the decline of mortgage rates through the three channels of improving market functioning, clarifying government support, and rebalancing portfolios. The purchase program improved market functioning, indicated by mortgage market participants re-entering the mortgage market after seeing that mortgage rate fluctuations decreased less and less. This helped participants gain confidence that the mortgage market was returning to normal. A decline in abnormal pricing for mortgages and MBS proved clearer government backing for the purchase program, as participants were more clear of the government's objectives in improving the mortgage markets, and thus were more confident in re-entering and participating in the mortgage markets. As a result, market participants were more willing to rebalance their portfolios and increase their MBS holdings due to their newfound confidence in the strength and stability of the mortgage market. All three channels combined created a downward pressure on mortgage rates, and as a result, mortgage rates decreased by a total of 139 basis points. This was consistent with their hypothesis that mortgage rates would decline by about 100 basis points and that the Federal Reserve's MBS purchase program would decrease mortgage rates.

Hancock and Passmore (2011) relate to Mian and Sufi (2014) when describing Fannie Mae and Freddie Mac as the most dominant players in the secondary mortgage market. Mian and Sufi

(2014) described how Fannie Mae and Freddie Mac bought mortgages from all over the country, pooled these mortgages together, and then sold them to investors as MBS. GSEs guaranteed these MBS, so investors were willing to pay a high price for these secured securities. As long as individuals that took out mortgages continued to make payments and avoided mortgage default, securitization was very profitable for both the GSEs and MBS investors. As the recession approached, more and more households defaulted on their mortgages, and the GSEs debt piled up. This related to Hancock and Passmore (2011), as they described how this GSE debt required a clearer government backing for Fannie Mae and Freddie Mac. Hancock and Passmore (2011) described how a clearer government backing for GSEs was needed to mitigate investor concerns about secured securities. A clearer government backing of the GSEs was crucial for investors because without GSE credibility investors would be very skeptical about purchasing MBS.

Although Hancock and Passmore (2011) presented their data very efficiently, there are two weaknesses that need to be addressed. First, Hollifield (2011) notes that when interpreting the changes in the relationship between mortgage rates and the different variables in the Hancock and Passmore (2011) regressions, one cannot assume that the Federal Reserve MBS program is the only variable driving the results. Although the results of the regressions did show that the MBS program leads to a change in correlation between the explanatory variable and mortgage rates, the data may not be completely accurate if one assumes all change is due to the MBS program. Second, Hancock and Passmore (2011) explained how once the Federal Reserve' MBS program stabilized the mortgage market there was continued downward pressure on mortgage rates. They briefly mentioned that this downward pressure dissipates in the first quarter of 2009, but did not expand on why this happened. Market confusion about what the MBS program's objectives were was a possibility, but the fact that the authors do not investigate the first quarter of 2009 deeper, results in a weakness of the article.

There are a few areas Hancock and Passmore (2011) could research further in order to enhance the article. First, one of the main goals of the Federal Reserve during this time period was to increase liquidity in the market. It would benefit the analysis if the authors provided a discussion about how the MBS program increased liquidity in the market through channels other than lower mortgage rates. Secondly, the analysis could be enhanced if Hancock and Passmore (2011) discussed how the economy would have suffered if the Federal Reserve did not intervene. It would have been very enlightening to understand how critical the MBS program was to the economy and what the result would have been if nothing were done. This research would involve looking at data and projecting future mortgage rates based on this data. This research would add a compelling outlook to the field and would provide further evidence supporting the importance of the Federal Reserve's MBS program.

## Multiple Choice Questions

1. According to Hancock and Passmore (2011), on November 25, 2008 the Federal Reserve put into place a program in which it purchased MBS. Which of the following is not one of the three channels in which the program decreased mortgage rates?
   (a) The program improved market functioning in both primary and secondary mortgage markets
   (b) The program showed a clearer government backing for Fannie Mae and Freddie Mac (GSEs)
   (c) The program provided anticipation of portfolio rebalancing effects
   **(d) The program provided banks funds to lend to subprime home buyers**

**Explanation:** The correct answer is (d): The program provided banks funds to lend to subprime home buyers. The Federal Reserve purchased up to $500 billion in MBSs in an attempt to lower mortgage rates through three channels. The first channel that lowered mortgage rates was the idea that the program improved market functioning in both primary and secondary mortgage markets.

This channel signals to market participants that, despite market conditions, there would be a MBS purchaser in the secondary market that could be relied on. The second channel is that the program showed a clear government backing for Fannie Mae and Freddie Mac. This was important because investors no longer had to be concerned about the value of the implicit government guarantee against credit risk. The third channel in which the mortgage rates were lowered was through the anticipation of portfolio rebalancing effects. The program expected people to adjust the assets in which they were investing in and in turn lower the mortgage rates.

2. According to Hancock and Passmore (2011), on September 7, 2008 the FHFA placed Fannie Mae and Freddie Mac into conservatorship. Which of the following were steps taken by the Treasury that complemented FHFA's decision to place Fannie Mae and Freddie Mac into conservatorship?

   (a) The Treasury and FHFA established Preferred Stock Purchase Agreements — contractual agreements between the Treasury and the conserved entities to ensure that each company would maintain a positive net worth

   (b) The Treasury established a new secured lending credit facility that would be available to Freddie Mac, Fannie Mae, and the Federal Home Loan banks

   (c) The Treasury initiated a temporary program to purchase GSEs' MBS

   (d) (b) and (c)

   **(e) All of the above**

**Explanation:** The answer is (e): One step taken by the Treasury to complement the conservatorship decision was the establishment of Preferred Stock Purchase Agreements. These contractual agreements between the Treasury and the GSEs allowed them to maintain a positive net worth. A second step taken by the Treasury was the establishment of a new secured lending credit facility that would be available to the GSEs. This establishment provided a temporary liquidity backstop authority that was crucial during this period. A third step taken by the Treasury was the implementation of a program to purchase GSE MBS.

3. According to Hancock and Passmore (2011), which of the following is false?

(a) Mortgage market analysts generally praised the Federal Reserve MBS purchase program when it was announced

(b) The Federal Reserve MBS purchase program resolved problems such as illiquidity, price discovery, and ambiguity about the government guarantees in the secondary mortgage market

(c) There was a fairly long delay between the announcement of, and implementation of, the Federal Reserve's intervention into MBS

**(d) The Federal Reserve MBS purchase program was not praised by market participants when it was introduced**

**Explanation:** The answer is (d): The Federal Reserve MBS purchase program was not praised by market participants when it was introduced. The first statement is true, as the MBS purchase program was praised by market analysts when it was first announced. Analysts believed that this program was an important statement by the government to show their support for the market. The implementation of the program resolved many problems in the market such as illiquidity, price discovery and the ambiguity about government guarantees in the secondary mortgage market. Although the system was strongly supported, there was a fairly long delay between the announcement and implementation of the Federal Reserve's intervention into MBS markets. The MBS purchase program was in fact praised by market participants when it was introduced.

## References

Hancock, D. and W. Passmore (2011), "Did the Federal Reserve's MBS Purchase Program Lower Mortgage Rates?", *Journal of Monetary Economics* 58, 498–514.

Hollifield, B. (2011), "Comments on 'Did the Federal Reserve's MBS Purchase Program Lower Mortgage Rates?'", *Journal of Monetary Economics* 58, 515–517.

Jickling, M. (2008), "Fannie Mae and Freddie Mac in Conservatorship." *Congressional Research Service*, Library of Congress.

Mian, A. and A. Sufi (2014), *House of Debt*, USA: The University of Chicago Press.

Stroebel, J. C., and J. B. Taylor (2012), "Estimated Impact of the Fed's Mortgage-Backed Securities Purchase Program", *International Journal of Central Banking* 8, 1–42.

# Chapter 18
# Supply of Mortgage Credit

*In collaboration with* Austin Reif and Jacob Hall

If someone was asked how much securitized home mortgage debt was backed by government sponsored enterprises (GSEs) in 2007, one would probably say, "What's a GSE?" instead of the correct answer — $4 trillion — an amount nearly doubling the sum of all outstanding consumer debt in the U.S. While this is an impressive figure, it might still be difficult to fully understand its meaning without first understanding what a GSE is. A GSE is a government sponsored enterprise, first created in 1970 by the U.S. Department of Housing and Urban Development to help reduce local bank's exposure to local market risks through securitization. Securitization was a way for banks to pool mortgages together to create a safer bundle of mortgages to then, in turn, sell those mortgage bundles to the secondary mortgage market. This is where GSEs come into play. The GSEs bought the mortgage bundles from banks. However, the GSE would not just purchase any mortgage bundle, they insured themselves from purchasing poor-quality bundles by requiring limits on loan sizes and loan-to-value (LTV) ratios. At the beginning of the subprime mortgage crisis, the two most popular GSEs — Fannie Mae and Freddie Mac — were heavily involved in the secondary mortgage market, purchasing mortgages from banks that dealt primarily with lower income families in urban residential areas. As the financial crisis peaked, more and more Americans were unable to meet their required mortgage payments. Fannie Mae and Freddie Mac, left without their primary source of income, turned to the U.S. government for assistance.

With regard to this framework, this chapter will discuss the rise, decline, and rise again of the GSEs and their potential crowd out effects in the context of the Gabriel and Rosenthal's (2010) analysis of information released through the Home Mortgage Disclosure Act and the 1990 and 2000 censuses. However, before proceeding any further, here is a definition of crowding out. Crowding out is the phenomenon that occurs when increased government involvement in a market affects the remainder market, essentially pushing their competition to the edges of the market. This chapter will show that GSEs were in fact more boon than bane to the secondary mortgage market, despite potentially facilitating the crowding out of private-label securities by summarizing the data from Gabriel and Rosenthal (2010).

Gabriel and Rosenthal (2010) began their investigation of the potential crowd out effect by first exploring HMDA data from 1994 to 2008. This information would provide a backdrop for their crowd out model. From 1994 to 2008, they gathered home purchase loans and refinancing information of GSEs and non-GSEs. As one would expect, their findings showed that in 1994 lenders were strongly reliant on local depositors as a means to supply funds. GSEs and private-labels combined only created 52 percent of originations for home loan purchases, but this changed over the course of the 1990s and 2000s as purchase-to-originations rose to 100 percent in 2004 and stayed at this rate until the financial crisis. Shockingly, most of the capital used today for conventional conforming sized home loans are from the secondary market, a drastic change from 20 years ago. Prior to 2004, GSEs created most of the secondary market for home purchasing and home refinancing. This is because prior to 2004, private-labels rarely used securitization. Once private-labels began securitization, they did not take the same precautions as GSEs. Private-labels extended credit to those who should not have received credit, what will be defined as a marginal borrower, and sold their securitized mortgages at alarming rates. This is what created the rapid increase of private-labels compared to GSEs from 2004 to 2007.

Gabriel and Rosenthal (2010) also examined data from the U.S. census in order to control socioeconomic status by using variables such as race, sex, education, unemployment, population density, medium income, and medium income of the metropolitan area. This is so their model would be as accurate and controlled as possible. There is one issue even with the controls that Gabriel and Rosenthal mentioned: the possibility that an unobserved trait that generates GSE purchases also generates private-label purchases. This would create a downward bias of the crowd out effect and create a lower bound estimate to the extent of the possible GSE crowd out. Knowing this weakness, Gabriel and Rosenthal combated this externality by creating a new trait called the "underserved status." They used the definition provided by Congress under the Federal Housing Enterprise Financial Safety and Soundness Act of 1992. A family qualifies as underserved if their median family income is less than 90 percent of the area median income (AMI), or between 90 percent and 120 percent of the AMI with over 30 percent of the population being African American or Hispanic. This act required a hefty amount of GSE loan purchases be made up of loans issued to borrowers that reside in an underserved census tract and/or of low-income status. To be considered low-moderate income, one's income must be less than the AMI. In 2008, when the government over-took Fannie Mae and Freddie Mac, over 55 percent of loans purchased were issued to low-moderate income borrowers while 39 percent of loans were required to have been issued to people who qualified in the "underserved" census status. This data, in conjunction with data from other studies discussed in Gabriel and Rosenthal (2010), showed that the GSEs were doing exactly what GSEs were meant to do. This is significant because not only were GSEs helping out the low-moderate income families, they were doing so responsibly, unlike what the private-labels began to do in the mid-2000s. As stated before, the GSEs had to have limits and strict requirements in order to ensure a safe securitization.

Imagine a scenario which, although fictitious for the purposes of this chapter, was all too real for many Americans not too long ago: after years of saving, the Johnson family had finally put enough money away to move out of their inner-city apartment and into a house in a suburban neighborhood. After months of witnessing their neighbors getting credit and the continuous rise of house values, the Johnsons decided to get a mortgage on their new home from a private-label. Little did they know, their mortgage would be securitized and pooled with many other marginal borrowers. The firm that financed and bundled these mortgages would then turn around and sell them on the secondary mortgage market, washing their hands of the Johnsons and the other families whose mortgages had been securitized. When the financial crisis hit, the Johnsons and many others began to fall behind on their payments. Neighborhoods became littered with foreclosure signs and the Johnsons, like many other families, were forced to move out of the comfort of their homes and into low-cost and affordable housing. The firms that had bought their mortgages on the secondary market, suddenly unable to collect millions of dollars, were facing bankruptcy. If the private-labels would have been as responsible as the GSEs, this entire catastrophe could have been avoided.

This example exposes the irresponsibility of the private-labels and the practice of securitization. This tactic yielded high profits for the private-labels between 2004 and 2006, as seen in the rapid growth of the private-labels in Gabriel's and Rosenthal's data. Once the economy took a sharp downward turn and the housing bubble burst, their ill-advised strategy backfired. The data show the trend of mortgages financed by private-labels falling equal to GSEs in 2007 and below GSEs in 2008. This of course is because of the collapse of the housing market. As an increasing portion of the American population fell into economic conditions qualifying them for underserved status in the eyes of the GSEs, more and more mortgages began to be financed through GSEs including: Fannie Mae and Freddie Mac.

Gabriel and Rosenthal (2010) used a simple model that shows the necessary market conditions for GSE loan purchases that would likely crowd out purchases by private-labels in the secondary market. They assumed that higher purchase prices, which induced lenders in the primary market to supply more loans, would make a relatively elastic supply function. Gabriel and Rosenthal state that the supply increase is due to lenders originating more loans and because the lenders may sell a greater share of portfolio loans. Another assumption they made was that the loan supply function would become more inelastic as loan supply increased. This is because loans held in portfolio by the main leaders would be highly valued and the most valued loans would be sold first. The secondary market loan demand would cross the elastic supply function and demand would increase with GSEs. This would create a price increase which would make lenders in the primary market more willing to supply loans to the secondary market. In this model, the GSE crowd out of private-labels would be very limited according to Gabriel and Rosenthal. If the demand would intersect loan supply at an inelastic part of the secondary market, then the crowd out would be more noticeable. This is because the price of the loans is higher, but also the number of loans on the secondary market would hardly increase compared to the first example. Gabriel and Rosenthal (2010) showed that crowd out from GSEs is higher when the demand for loan purchases is high and when the secondary market has an inelastic loan supply. Crowd out is reduced when demand crosses at an elastic section of the supply curve.

After exploring the background data and setting up the model, Gabriel and Rosenthal (2010) showed evidence of a very limited GSE crowd out from 1994 to 2001 in the home loan market. This was to be expected because private-labels did not begin mass securitization until 2002. The peak of GSE crowd out ranged about 45–50 percent in 2005, but then vanished in 2007 and 2008 during the financial crisis. This was expected because of the intense drop off in private-label loans. Gabriel and Rosenthal also stated that these trends are identical yet more sensitive in the house refinancing markets. Crowd out was the most noticeable when market activity was high, for example in 2004–2006, and smaller in less active periods, such as, the mid 1990–2003 and 2007–2008. Furthermore, they showed that the 2008 government appropriation of Fannie Mae and Freddie Mac played a vital role in sustaining home mortgage credit flow during the Great Recession.

Gabriel and Rosenthal (2010) concluded that if it were not for the government takeover of GSEs, the mortgage lending market — and with it the housing market — would have suffered even greater damages than it already had. Due to the risky practices of private-label firms, the secondary mortgage market was in shambles. Fannie Mae and Freddie Mac provided necessary mortgage credit to millions of Americans that otherwise would have been forced into foreclosure or left unable to finance their homes.

The data that Gabriel and Rosenthal (2010) used in their model was reminiscent of the ideas portrayed in Mian and Sufi's book about the recent financial crisis. Mian and Sufi (2014) explain the multiple views on why the Great Recession was caused and look empirically and historically at data to eliminate various arguments. The data represented in Gabriel and Rosenthal (2010) connects with what Mian and Sufi (2014) said about private-label securities and their rise and fall. Mian and Sufi showed that private-label securitization directly encouraged irresponsible lending by showing that if someone had a credit score of 620 that meant that person had a higher probability of defaulting than someone else with a credit score below 620. This was because a person with a credit score of 620 would be securitized. Even though the data from Gabriel and Rosenthal (2010) did not blatantly show the effects of private-label securitizations, one could still see the trends occurring. Comparing those trends with what was happening in America at the time, allows one to see the correlation with the rises and falls of the private-label securitization and understand why those rises and falls occurred.

One potential weakness that Gabriel and Rosenthal (2010) has is that while the data provided an in-depth look at how the government bailout helped GSEs, it did not get into how firms such as banks and private-labels that also received bailout money were affected. One can see how government appropriation significantly helped the GSEs bounce back from the recession and confidently re-enter the secondary mortgage market, but it would be interesting to examine how private companies fared in comparison to

GSEs. Knowing the answer to this question could allow for better speculation into how relevant GSEs would be in the future.

Some suggestions for future research would be to see how relevant GSEs are today in the current recovering economy. Is the mortgage market still as weak as it was in the 1970s that would warrant the continuation of GSEs? Would the U.S. economy be better off with responsible private-label securitization or are GSEs a necessity to ensure responsible securitization? However, one thing is certain and that is the government bailout of Fannie Mae and Freddie Mac was a net-positive to keep a flow of house credit going during the financial crisis.

## Multiple Choice Questions

1. According to Gabriel and Rosenthal (2010), GSEs and private-labels combined to make up what percent of originations for home loan purchases in 1994?
   (a) 39 percent
   (b) 72 percent
   **(c) 52 percent**
   (d) 26 percent

**Explanation:** The correct answer is (c): At this time, local depositors were heavily relied on for originations for home loan purchases. Only one decade later however, purchase-to-originations jumped to 100 percent and stayed at this level until 2008 when the financial crisis hit. This is because of the influx of private-label firms using securitization. Once both GSEs and private-labels began using securitization, local depositors played a much smaller part in the mortgage finance market as the secondary mortgage market expanded.

2. According to Gabriel and Rosenthal (2010), what does AMI stand for in the context of GSEs and the underserved status designation?
   (a) Average Median Income
   (b) **Area Median Income**
   (c) Area Mean Income
   (d) Average Metropolitan Income

**Explanation:** The correct answer is (b): In order for a family to have underserved status, they must have a household income that is under 90 percent of the AMI. If over 30 percent of the metropolitan statistical area that the family resides in is African American or Hispanic, the household's income must be between 90 percent and 120 percent of the AMI. This statistic is extremely useful because it allows GSEs to examine each mortgage loan applicant in respect to the other applicants in their area, giving a sense as to the most deserving households.

3. What percent of Fannie Mae and Freddie Mac loans were required to be issued to households deemed as underserved according to Gabriel and Rosenthal (2010)?

   **(a) 39 percent**
   (b) 55 percent
   (c) 63 percent
   (d) 25 percent

**Explanation:** The correct answer is (a): This is significant not just because the GSEs were serving a part of the population that often did not have as good of credit as more well-to-do Americans, but because the number of households that achieved underserved status spiked after the financial collapse. Many households that only a couple years prior would have been able to choose from a wide range of mortgages were now severely limited. The GSEs offered them loans with affordable plans once they were considered underserved.

## References

Mian, A. and A. Sufi (2014), *House of Debt*, USA: The University of Chicago Press.

Gabriel, S. and S. Rosenthal (2010), "Do the GSEs Expand the Supply of Mortgage Credit? New Evidence of Crowd Out in the Secondary Mortgage Market", *Journal of Public Economics* 94, 975–986.

# Chapter 19

# The Home Affordable Modification Program

*In collaboration with* Kelsey Gallivan
and Christopher Colombe

Ensuing the drastic spike in foreclosures, which was initiated in 2008, housing prices plummeted and the housing market faced a dire need to deal with foreclosures in a way that would help to prevent them. The federal government intervened with targeting foreclosure avoidance. Understanding the rationale behind this policy is essential in our analysis of governments' role in the economy as more than just a regulatory body, but as an institution responsible for implementing reactionary measures to catastrophic events such as the subprime mortgage crisis.

By the first quarter of 2011, Home Affordable Modification Program (HAMP) had introduced over 1.5 million trial modifications and 670,000 permanent modifications. The HAMP is one of the most important programs initiated and has helped to promote loan modifications. So why would the government want to intervene? Primarily, it was to identify value-enhancing loans that would be good candidates for modifications that included payment-reduction. HAMP was one of the primary programs installed that would assess the value of current loans risking default and ultimately make a determination as to whether a mortgage modification would in fact be "value-improving" for investors.

As Holden *et al.* (2012) says, "A loan that is net present value "positive", where the value of the probability-weighted mod cash flows exceed the value of the probability-weighted no-mod cash flows, is considered to be a good candidate for modification." It should be noted that the goal of HAMP, although often benefited by the borrower, was spurred by appealing to the investor or lender to forgo foreclosure and provide modification to the borrower. The program provides subsidies to lenders that are willing to make modifications upon mortgages. HAMP, however, helped the housing market to evade a significant number of foreclosures.

Overall, the goal of HAMP was essentially to reduce the number of foreclosures throughout the U.S. The benefits are oftentimes more easily seen but Holden *et al.* (2012) attempts to analyze drawbacks, while also providing the framework for how these loans were adjusted and the incentives provided through subsidy to mortgage owners.

Within their paper, Holden *et al.* (2012) provide data supporting correlations between specific key loan characteristics or inputs and the probability of foreclosures. Their model essentially analyzes whether or not the mortgage is worth making modifications through analyzing and valuing the net present value (NPV) that is created through modification. Their model primarily takes into consideration information pertaining to the borrower and several borrower characteristics including the debt-to-income ratio, Fair Isaac Corporation (FICO), as well as the market-to-market loan-to-value (MTMLTV). The criteria are designed to be the decision-making framework in determining whether a modification should be extended to the borrower. Generally, the goal of the average HAMP modification is to reduce default probability by lowering the LTV ratio and mortgage payment. The change in default probability is what contributes to the increase in value for the investor most significantly. Therefore, a change in default probability from 90 percent to 60 percent would have more value than a 5 percent reduction from 20 to 15 even though the latter has the ultimate lowest default risk. A mortgage with high re-default risk following modification may still be worth the cost, as long as the decrease in re-default risk equals the amount of cost through modification. A mortgage with a high initial default risk will have the most to gain.

The criteria including debt-to-income, FICO, and MTMLTV are strong indicators of the potential value added from modification. Default rates tend to decrease with lower debt-to-income of the borrower. The desired debt-to-income ratio provided by HAMP aims at 31 percent. Oftentimes, if the front end starting debt-to-income is too high, above 38 percent, NPV will begin to decline because the modification will require too substantial of monthly payment reductions. The target range of starting debt-to-income to successfully decrease debt-to-income eventually appears to be between 31 and 38 percent. On the other hand, if the starting debt-to-income is too low, such as below 31 percent, then the modification will be costlier than the value added. Essentially, the reduction in payments will be greater than the value added and result in negative NPV. Therefore, that range between 31 percent and 38 percent is ideal. Holden *et al.* (2012) also indicated that FICO scores and the MTMLTV are highly correlated with the default rate. The default rate increases with MTMLTV while it decreases with FICO Scores.

After a time of increased default and decline in housing prices, the goal of HAMP was to produce a model that could provide the government with a way to successfully modify loan structures. The use of the HAMP NPV model has been a successful foundation to achieve this goal and to help identify and predict borrowers' default behavior. Using the four static paths provides a systematic and simple way to determine whether a modification is NPV positive and would be beneficial to restructure from a lender's point of view. The model is successful in its responsiveness to characteristics such as FICO scores and debt-to-income ratios. In order for this responsiveness to be successful, the model had to be formed on a number of assumptions, one of the model's biggest constraints. There is evidence that the HAMP NPV model is able to predict some borrowers' risk of default, but the question relies on if this is the most effective method today. As time goes on, and more data and models become available, Holden *et al.* (2012) argues that the loan modification process will lead to better outcomes for homeowners, servicers, and lenders.

In the now famous book, "House of Debt" Mian and Sufi discuss how hard cut-offs are not necessarily indicative of reality. Mian and Sufi (2014) discuss one study where it was hypothesized that mortgages under a 620 credit score were less likely to be accepted into a mortgage-backed security pool and the scores above 620 were more likely to be accepted. It would make sense that borrowers with a credit score above 620 would have a lower probability of default and the borrowers slightly below 620 would have a higher probability of default. Mian and Sufi's book explains the opposite as it turned out that borrowers with credit scores just below 620 had lower default rates than the borrowers with a credit score just above 620.

This is something to keep in mind when looking at the HAMP NPV model Holden *et al.* (2012) discuss. The HAMP NPV model is based on assumptions and relies heavily on cut offs when deciding if a borrower will be qualified for a modification. Credit scores are one of the factors used in evaluating if a modification will be NPV positive. These cut offs may be a good starting point but may not be indicative of what is happening in reality.

Although the HAMP NPV model is shown to provide a uniform way to evaluate loans that could be in trouble, it is a relatively a new model that heavily relies on many assumptions. For the model to be simple and easy for many servicers to use, it uses only information readily available, which in turn is something that could lead to adverse selection. Original underwriting processes and other financial obligations were not used since they are not available for all borrowers. This severely limits the ability of the NPV model to take into account other factors that could affect a borrower's probability of default, instead of just looking at a select few factors such as FICO scores and LTV ratios.

Another limitation of Holden *et al.* (2012) article is how the HAMP NPV model affects borrowers. When the federal government formed the model, its goal was to assess whether a loan modification would be beneficial from the lender's point of view. The question then arises what the consequences will be for the borrower if the loan is only modified to benefit the lender. Holden *et al.* (2012) rarely focuses on how the NPV pass test impacts borrowers and more heavily focuses on the benefits it provides to lenders.

With that being said, further research could be done on how defaulters are affected. Since the model is relatively new, research could be done to see if there is a more inclusive model that focuses on the lender's needs while also focusing on the borrower's needs. It would be beneficial to obtain significant statistics on how the HAMP NPV model impacts debtors. On top of this, it would also be helpful to include data on the financial impact to both mortgagors and mortgagees in the no modification situation. Since the model has only been implemented within the past seven years, exploration could be done on how the HAMP NPV model will change in the future.

## Multiple Choice Questions

1. According to Holden *et al.* (2012), for a modification to generate a NPV positive result what must happen?
   (a) The cost of the modification must be recovered by a decrease in the probability of avoiding a costly foreclosure
   (b) The cost of the modification must be maintained by a stable probability of avoiding a costly foreclosure
   **(c) The cost of the modification must be recovered by an increase in the probability of avoiding a costly foreclosure**
   (d) The cost of the modification must be recovered by decrease of the probability of a costly foreclosure

**Explanation:** The first step in finding the cost of modification is finding the probability that the borrower will not default without the modification. This probability is then multiplied by the change in cash flows from the unmodified loan cures to the modified loan cures. In order for this to be recovered and generate a positive NPV, firstly the cost of making the modification must be less than the reduction of the probability of default caused by the modification. This is then multiplied by the expected losses occurred from default to generate a positive NPV.

2. According to Holden *et al.* (2012) what is the one characteristic associated with a higher NPV pass rate?

    (a) Loans that require greater financial concessions
    (b) Loans with large amounts of principal forbearance
    (c) Loans with a high initial front-end DTI
    **(d) Loans at higher risk of default**

**Explanation:** Loans that are at a higher risk of default are more likely to be beneficial to modify from the lender's perspective and thus are more likely to be categorized as NPV pass. A low probability of foreclosure would be less likely to cause financial stress on the lender and thus is more likely to not be as beneficial to modify. Although the costs of the modification can be higher and offset a decreased probability of foreclosure, generally loans that are at a higher risk of default are one characteristic of an NPV pass due to the financial burden it can bring to mortgagees.

3. According to Holden *et al.* (2012), for a borrower with negative equity:

    **(a) The NPV is generally increasing with respect to FICO scores**
    (b) FICO scores increase as NPV increases
    (c) NPV decreases with respect to FICO scores
    (d) There is no association between NPV and FICO scores

**Explanation:** FICO scores affect the NPV calculations on prepayment and default models. When borrowers have a lot of equity their losses are not predicted to be very high. NPV does not change much due to the low differences in probabilities of default. The opposite is true for when borrowers have negative equity. When a borrower has negative equity, their losses are expected to be higher. There is an increase in the difference between the unmodified loan and modified loan, causing a changing or increasing NPV.

# References

Holden S., A. Kelly, D. McManus, T. Scharlemann, R. Singer and J. Worth (2012), "The HAMP NPV Model: Development and Early Performance", *Real Estate Economics* 40, S32–S64.

Mian, A. and A. Sufi (2014), *House of Debt*, USA: The University of Chicago Press.

# Part IV
# House Prices and Lending Standards

# Chapter 20

# Home Equity-Based Borrowing

*In collaboration with* Mark Nicola
and John Kliewer

The beginning of the 21st century was a very prosperous time. This was a period in which there was a great increase in technological advancement. A period in which individuals had more technology on their phones than there was in the space shuttle during the first Apollo space mission. This was the first decade in which a computer was in almost every American home and we had the ability to access copious amount of information with the click of a mouse. There was also a change in the financial sector. Individuals were saving much less and spending more. This period mirrored the roaring twenties in which people were racking up debt. As the roaring twenties had a huge economic downturn leading to the worst economic crisis in U.S. history in the Great Depression, this period of great prosperity at the beginning of the new century also had a hard economic downturn as well, one that rivaled that of Great Depression.

One of the main factors involved in this economic downturn was the negative effect on the housing market and more specifically a decrease in housing prices and how it interacted with the economy. Mian and Sufi (2011) look specifically at this and try to explain it. The goals of their study were to see how borrowing by homeowners changed in response to a change in house prices and to look at which set of homeowners reacted harshest.

The data used was from Equifax, which is one of the three largest credit reporting agency in the United States. The collected information came from 74,149 homeowners across 2,307 ZIP codes throughout 68 metropolitan statistical areas (MSAs). This was a subset of the initial sample which included 266,005 individuals. This information was used to split them into three groups. The first group, which encompassed 34 percent, contained people who currently have a mortgage or home equity debt. The second group, which included 8 percent, did not have a mortgage currently, but had one at some point within the last year. The third group, which included the last 58 percent of people, did not currently have a mortgage and had not had a mortgage in the past year. They used these groupings to determine homeownership because the data from Equifax does not measure homeownership.

To add to the individual-level data, they added information from other data sets. This included Internal Revenue Service (IRS) income data, information from the Census Business Statistics regarding employment and payroll information, FCSW house price data, and also Equifax's consumer credit score data. IRS data is only available for 1998, 2002, 2003, 2005, and 2006, so the missing years are interpolated for data before 2006 and extrapolated for data after 2006.

For demographics, the 2000 decennial census was used for ZIP code level information. The measure of topology-based housing supply elasticity is from an article written by Saiz in 2010.

Sufi and Mian (2011) used three separate models to predict how homeowners, with all other variables being equal, responded to an increase in house prices. The first model is unconstrained long-lived homeowners. These individuals use housing consumption for their needs because they are not constrained due to debt. When house prices go up for these individuals, housing consumption becomes relatively more expensive, so there is zero tendency to borrow out of housing gains.

The second model deals with short-lived homeowners. They do not hold much merit in housing wealth and plan before death on consuming some of housing capital. These owners would borrow more due to an increase in housing prices. The older the individuals are, the more likely they are to borrow against their house due to a shorter period left they will be in that house.

The last model is credit constrained homeowners. They would like to borrow more in order to consume more but they are not able to due to their bad credit and little collateral. These homeowners borrow heavily with an increase in housing prices in order to consume more.

To test these models, Mian and Sufi (2011) used four separate strategies. The first strategy was the across MSA empirical approach. They looked at the differences in housing price growth, total debt growth, and change in debt to income ratio for both inelastic housing supply and elastic housing supply. Elastic supply is able to change quickly while inelastic is not. They found debt growth was 20 percent higher for housing prices and debt for inelastic supply and had a debt to income change that was 0.6 higher than elastic.

Then, Mian and Sufi (2011) looked to see if borrowing changed based on type of consumer. They found that debt growth was much higher for low credit quality homeowners, high credit card utilization when housing supply was inelastic. The 1997 credit score was a huge predictor of debt elasticity. Individuals one standard deviation below the debt mean had debt elasticity to home prices of 0.76 compared to a 0.35 to those owners one standard deviation above the mean. They did find a difference in age of homeowner and debt to income ratio but neither of these was found to have been statistically significant.

Mian and Sufi (2011) also looked at the exclusion restriction to determine if the differences in trends between inelastic and elastic MSA's could be due to anything other than housing prices. While there is no way to fully exclude all other variables, little to no evidence was found to suggest these trends were due to anything but housing prices. The fact that a greater prevalence of borrowing was found to be focused more in home related debt points to a home equity-based borrowing channel.

The last approach Mian and Sufi (2011) took was within MSA estimation strategy. This looks at a different source of variations in house prices compared to that of the across MSA strategy. Both strategies use local average treatment effect estimators with the average being computed for the exclusive parts of the home price distribution. Despite these two approaches using different data, the results were very similar, validating the authors work.

Mian and Sufi (2011) then looked at what this money borrowed was being used for. The results were that the majority of money borrowed was used for consumption purposes or home improvement. This matters because if the money was used to pay off other debts there would not be as large of an impact and the crisis may not have been as severe.

Mian and Sufi also look at how the credit quality of the homeowner and leverage the homeowner has in the house affects the chance of default. They found low credit homeowners had a much higher chance of defaulting. This was especially true for those homeowners in inelastic MSA's in which their default rate was approximately twice that of their elastic.

The first conclusion from Mian and Sufi (2011) was a large link between borrowing and housing prices. It allowed them to determine the type of borrower for whom the home equity-based borrowing channel is strongest. They showed that the individuals with low credit scores and high probability to use credit cards did the most borrowing. They found a correlation between borrowing and the price of houses that show that housing and leverage are a huge part in what is going on in the economy on a macroeconomic scale. They found that fluctuations in household leverage were good at predicting the recession between 2007 and 2009. This could possibly be used to predict future economic downturns.

These findings are reflective of those in Mian and Sufi (2014), as they concluded that the price of households impacts highly leveraged homeowners the most, especially those with low credit scores and a high tendency to borrow on credit cards. To maintain the economy, they suggest monitoring changes in household leverage at the county level because it will help to foresee the recession.

Mian and Sufi (2011) used evidence from studies to back up these arguments, but there are a couple possible weaknesses of the study. The population that was affected the most (low credit scores, high tendency to borrow) could be a result of self-control problems instead of household credit limitations as they acknowledge. The Equifax data measured individuals, not households, so they needed to sort through the data and determine what defines a homeowner in debt. This could cause some confusion and possible exclusion of some types of data. Another possible weakness is the exclusion restriction. They recognized the possibility that, "differential trends in inelastic and elastic MSAs during this time period would lead to differential borrowing patterns even in the absence of differential house price growth" (Mian, 2011). They concluded, however, for another factor to drive borrowing in inelastic MSAs, it would have to uniquely apply to their most concentrated group and drive them to leverage their house.

For further understanding of household borrowing and its impact on the economic recession of 2008, research should focus on running economic models to rule out the trends that could possibly be influencing borrowing. One example of a trend they could rule out is comparing liquidity restrictions and self-control problems. Their conclusion is specific enough to logically rule out trends, but it is not completely certain.

The next step that could be taken involves using the intuition that Mian and Sufi (2011) used in their paper to make an economic model from the results. This model would be extremely helpful for the future. It could be used to help predict future economic downturns when certain conditions are met. This could not only allow for society to have a relative idea when the economy is going to take a turn for the worst, but would also allow for society to takes steps, such as suggesting individuals to spend less and save more, to negate the severity of the economic crisis, perhaps stop it from happening completely.

## Multiple Choice Questions

1. According to Mian and Sufi (2011), home equity-based borrowing channel is not uniform across households. Homeowners
with _____ credit card utilization rates and _____ initial credit
scores have the strongest tendency to borrow against an increase
in home equity.

   (a) High; High
   (b) Low; High
   **(c) High; Low**
   (d) Low; Low

**Explanation:** The correct answer to this question is (c): Mian and
Sufi (2011) found "no effect of house prices on borrowing for homeowners in the top quartile of credit score distribution." This means
those who had a better credit score generally did not borrow as
much as those with worse credit scores did. From their paper, inelastic MSAs were much more affected by debt growth for high
credit card utilization. The elastic households in both low and high
credit card utilization functioned generally the same in terms of
debt growth. Therefore, if a homeowner used their credit card
regularly and had low credit scores, they were much more likely to
borrow against an increase in home equity.

2. According to Mian and Sufi (2011), _____ homeowners of both
inelastic and elastic MSAs were more likely to accumulate debt
between the years of 1998 and 2008.

   (a) Old
   (b) Young
   (c) Toddler
   **(d) None of the above**

**Explanation:** The correct answer is (d): There does seem to be a
difference between the young and old homeowners (with higher
debt growth for the younger ones), but Mian and Sufi explain that
debt growth is not significantly different between the two. They
hypothesized that older consumers would be more willing to

borrow because their home equity is higher and that they have a shorter time left on their equity, but that is not the case either.

3.  According to Mian and Sufi (2011), homeowners who borrow money against home equity tend to spend it on what?

    (a)  Pay off credit card or other debt
    **(b)  Consumption or home improvement**
    (c)  Buying real estate or financial assets
    (d)  A mix of all of the above

**Explanation:** The correct answer is (b): Most homeowners who borrow money against equity end up spending that money on goods or improving their household. The marginal return is high for borrowed funds, which explains why the economy further went into debt, as highly leveraged homeowners were able to spend less. This is the example in which there is no way that individuals borrow to pay off other debt. If they did the blow of economic downturns would be cushioned and would not be as severe.

## References

Mian, A. and A. Sufi (2011), "House Prices, Home Equity Borrowing, and the US Household Leverage Crisis", *American Economic Review* 101, 2132–2156.

Mian, A. and A. Sufi (2014), *House of Debt*, USA: The University of Chicago Press.

# Chapter 21

# Housing Prices During the Boom

*In collaboration with* Carly Manger and Andrew Hall

The increase in housing prices led consumer confidence in real estate investment to an irrational level, in which individuals felt that houses would continue their rise in value indefinitely. As credit expanded to subprime borrowers, homeownership became more than just a personal housing decision — it became a popular vehicle for investment. What were the causes of this surge in housing prices, and what role did they play in the overall development of the crisis? Understanding this linkage is essential to grasping the root causes of the housing bubble that preceded the imminent economic meltdown.

Throughout the housing boom in the early 2000, lower and middle class home buyers around the country, and specifically Illinois, artificially inflated transaction prices in order to gain a larger mortgage. Between 2005 and 2008, data show that up to 16 percent of highly leveraged transactions had inflated prices of up to 9 percent. These inflated transactions were common in financially constrained neighborhoods and when real estate professionals had an informational advantage. Those borrowers that inflated prices were more prone to default, although, their mortgage rates were not actually materially higher. Ben-David (2011) examines the circumstances in which inflated transactions occur and quantifies their correlations with home prices and mortgage performance.

The goal of Ben-David (2011) is to study the causes of the housing boom more closely; throughout his paper it becomes apparent that the increase in inflated transactions was a big factor. This inflation expanded the scope of transactions, including things such as appliances, transaction costs, cars, coupons, and cash, which made transaction prices seem higher to outside parties. This also allowed people to receive bigger mortgages based on the added value of these assets. Furthermore, these inflated transactions permitted real estate professionals to complete deals that would not have been possible due to the buyer's financial constraint.

There are two types of inflated transactions, legal but problematic transactions and illegal transactions. The legal transactions occur when lenders allow the transacting parties to include "seller concessions," such as transaction costs or a discount at the time of closing, in the price used to determine mortgage leverage. Lenders are legally bound to limit these concessions between 2 percent and 6 percent of the transaction price, and appraisers are required to provide fair value appraisals, cancelling out the effect of these concessions (Fannie Mae, 2005). However, appraisers tended to approve transaction prices as they were presented to them, allowing borrowers to use the inflated prices as a source for their mortgage borrowing (Aaron, 2006). Therefore, the observed price was higher than the true economic price. Due to the negative effect these concessions were having on transactions, the Federal Housing Administration (FHA) lowered the permitted seller concession from 6 percent of the transaction price to 3 percent in January 2010 (FHA, 2010).

The second type of inflated transaction is an illegal transaction. In these transactions, prices are inflated beyond what is approved by lenders and are considered mortgage fraud or "fraud for property." Moreover, these transactions generally included a concealed side transfer of cash or goods from the seller to the buyer. One example of this comes from Chicago in 2006, a builder offers to sell a condo for $235,000, but was willing to inflate the price to $255,000 and return $20,000 to the buyer, without disclosing the side payment to the lender. With this inflation of $20,000 the buyer was able to receive a 95 percent loan-to-value (LTV) mortgage with no down payment. The $242,250 loan was so large based on the inflated price that the buyer could have purchased this condo without investing any equity (Ben-David, 2011).

During the recent real estate boom, mortgage financing was not readily available to anyone. The rejection rate during this period was relatively high 35–50 percent Ho and Pennington-Cross, 2007; Zywicki and Adamson, 2008. Additionally, borrows who had low credit scores were not able to borrow at high leverage. The inflated transactions were identified using the Multiple Listing Service, a large database of property listings that include free descriptions of the property by sellers. The sample used by Ben-David (2011) consists of almost 800,000 residential transactions that comes from Cook County, Illinois between 1995 and 2008.

Artificially inflating prices is a common practice utilized to increase financially constrained potential buyers' demand. In a series of interviews conducted by Ben-David (2011), he was able to identify techniques utilized to inflate transaction prices. Ben-David (2011) interviewed a variety of real estate professionals including real estate agents, loan officers, appraisers, and real estate lawyers. They found that the borrower essentially borrows against things such as transaction costs that cannot be foreclosed upon by the lender. Effectively, the seller and buyer expand the scope of the transaction and sign a contract for a greater amount than the true economic value of the physical property. The buyer then uses the inflated sales contract in his or her mortgage application, and the appraiser verifies that the price is reasonable. Since mortgage amounts are determined as a fraction of the selling price, if the mortgage is approved then it is larger than it would have otherwise been.

The judgment of appraisers is one potential obstacle to inflating transactions. Under common appraisal rules, appraisers are instructed to value homes as if they were purchased for cash, with no other incentives to the buyer (Fannie Mae, 2005, 2007). However, the appraiser's incentives can be distorted. Since mortgage brokers generally appointed them, an incentive was created to approve inflated transaction prices in order to satisfy the broker and be called for future appraisal assignments. Although, the findings from the interviews show that in many cases appraisers were unaware of the inflated price, and many times knew not what to ask. Furthermore, until 2007, many appraisers were not very concerned with prices seeming too high, because the general level of house prices was increasing as well.

In order to test for the inflated transactions, Ben-David (2011) used two different data sets: the Cook County Recorder of Deeds and the Multiple Listings Service. The first data set includes information about all real-estate transactions in Cook County, Illinois from 1990 to present. The Multiple Listings Service includes all property listings and transactions that were recorded in Cook County from January 1995 through April 2008. In using these databases in his study, Ben-David removed transactions that most likely reflected data errors. Examples include transactions with extreme prices and transactions that were closed below 50 percent or above 200 percent of the listing price, among others.

Ben-David (2011) explained that a key feature of inflated transactions is that the side payment, which is what inflates the price, is unobservable. Therefore, in order to analyze this issue, it is required to find a variable that is correlated with this existence of side payments between the seller and buyer. Ben-David found that sellers were often explicitly hinting that they were willing to expand the scope of the transaction. Examples included stating, "$8,000 cash back to buyer with full price offer" or "no money down ....$10,000 under-appraised." To investigate the relationship of inflated transactions and side payments, Ben-David composed a list of word combinations that were likely to be associated with side payments but would be less common in other contexts. These combinations did not include anything that would have suggested improvements in the quality for the home for say, which would actually justify an increase in the price. A transaction that includes any of the combinations was then flagged with the variable *seller hint*. Overall, Ben-David (2011) found that 2.9 percent of transactions contained such hints. In mortgages with leverage above 80 percent, 3.4 percent were flagged and mortgages with leverage higher than 95 percent, 4.3 percent were flagged.

Ben-David (2011) began his empirical analysis by testing whether inflated transactions do indeed have higher prices. In order to do this, by looking at a property that has been transacted multiple times over the sample period, he calculated the difference in prices for each two consecutive transactions on the same property, and then compared the differences in prices across properties. If a seller hint was present in one of the transactions, it would bias the price of the specific transaction upward compared to the price of the other transaction on the same property. The results showed that when sellers hint about their willingness to provide a side payment, prices are higher by up to 5.3 percent, where the effect generally increased with leverage. In order to further confirm the existence of the seller's hint variable, Ben-David used different levels on geographical controls, as the research of Mian and Sufi showed that financial constraints have a strong association with geographic location (Mian and Sufi, 2009). Using these controls, he found an even stronger correlation with the effect of the seller hint variable as properties were inflated by up to 6.6 percent.

After establishing the existence of higher prices in inflated transactions, Ben-David (2011) then investigated the drivers of these transactions. These included the transactions occurring when the buyer is constrained and otherwise would not be able to complete the transaction, whether the frequency of transactions increased with financial constraints and overtime, and whether the likelihood of engaging in an inflated transaction increases with the stake that the intermediary has in the transaction. He relied on Erik Hurst and Frank Stafford to distinguished the financially constrained as those who have mortgages that are larger than 80 percent of their home value (Hurst and Stafford, 2004). This issue also directly relates to the research done by Mian and Sufi (2014) as the availability of subprime mortgages drastically increased in the early 2000s. Specifically, low credit-score ZIP codes in Chicago saw mortgages for home purchase grow by 36 percent per year from 2002 to 2005 (Mian and Sufi, 2014). He found that below 80 percent leverage, the percentage of transactions with seller hints is only 2 percent, with an increase to 4.9 percent with 100 percent leverage. Additionally, he found that a borrower who takes a 100 percent

LTV mortgage is 23 percent more likely to buy from a seller who has seller hints. He also found that transactions with seller hints increase over time, especially for the highly leveraged population. Next, he researched the role in intermediaries, including real estate agents and mortgage brokers. These intermediaries have different incentives that might make them more likely to facilitate inflated transactions. For example, real estate agents working on behalf of a seller generally receive 6 percent of the transaction amount (Levitt and Syverson, 2008). His results found that seller hints are indeed more prevalent when intermediaries have special incentives. Specifically, these agencies increased the likelihood of a seller hint transaction between 0.3 percent and 1.5 percent.

After determining that the inflated transactions have higher prices and that borrowers in these transactions have higher leverage than is perceived, Ben-David (2011) examined whether these borrowers were more likely to default and whether they had higher interest rates. He showed that the likelihood of foreclosure within one year for a borrower with 95–100 percent leverage who bought a property with seller hints was 0.6 percent more likely to default than a similar buyer without seller hints. In regard to interest rates, borrowers with LTV between 95 percent and 100 percent who bought with seller hints paid interest rates that were higher by 0.05–0.27 percent. Ben-David (2011) stated that these do not seem to reflect the risk that increases with more leverage.

Lastly, Ben-David (2011) discussed the aggregate affect that inflated prices have on overall market prices. In particular, buyers, sellers, and appraisers who look at recent transaction prices in the area may be misled by inflated prices. Results showed that prices in areas with prior intense price inflation tended to be higher by around 1.2 percent in the next quarter. Also, if inflated prices do occur and market participants (sellers, buyers, appraisers) do base their valuation estimates on comparable properties, then we should see prices having a larger distribution. Ben-David used standard deviation to show that this does indeed happen; that the standard deviation of prices increases in quarters that follow a high level of price inflation activity.

In conclusion, the evidence in this paper suggests that inflated transactions do in fact play a role in the financing of those who are financially constrained. For those who would not normally qualify for a mortgage, price inflation may be the only way they can become homeowners. For those who are not financially constrained, price inflation can effectively reduce monthly payments by increasing the value component of the LTV ratio. Between 2005 and early 2008, inflated transfers accounted for 4–9 percent of transactions with leverage higher than 80 percent. Next, intermediaries play a special role in this issue. They have the incentive to participate in inflating prices due to rewards in finishing transactions and know how to attract financially constrained buyers. Price inflation then had a detrimental effect on mortgage performance. Despite the fact of higher leverage and default risks, those who borrowed through inflated transactions paid the same interest rate. Lenders benefitted from inflated transactions because the market opened up to borrowers who could not originally afford/qualify for a mortgage.

The only potential weakness of the paper is the need for clearer explanations. For example, it is a confusing to figure out exactly what Ben-David (2011) is talking about in regard to seller's hints. It would be beneficial if he explicitly stated the definition as well as examples of a seller hint early on in the paper. In regard to the future, it would be beneficial to expand this research out of Cook County, Illinois and see if there are any effects geographically on this specific issue of seller hints and inflated transactions.

## Multiple Choice Questions

1. According to Ben-David (2011), in January 2010, the FHA lowered the seller concessions from 6 percent of the transaction price to which of the following?
   (a) 4 percent
   (b) 2 percent
   **(c) 3 percent**
   (d) 2.5 percent
   (e) None of the above

**Explanation:** The correct answer is (c): Ben-David (2011) explains that in legal inflated transactions, when these concessions are disclosed to the lender, most lenders limited concessions to 2–6 percent. Prior to the housing boom, there was never a large enough issue with inflated transactions such that the FHA needed to take action. In 2010, after the boom had busted, the FHA realized that something needed to be done, and therefore, lowered the allowed seller concessions from 6 percent of the transaction price down to 3 percent.

2. According to Ben-David (2011), inflated transactions are most likely to occur in which of the following?
   (a) Low-price properties and average-income neighborhoods, presumably where there is a large amount of diversity
   **(b) Low-price properties and low-income neighborhoods, presumably where financial constraints are more binding**
   (c) Low-price properties and high-income neighborhoods, presumably where price manipulation did not raise any flags
   (d) Low-price properties and low-income neighborhoods, presumably where buyers worked on average did 2–3 jobs

**Explanation:** The correct answer is (b): In the paper, Ben-David (2011) concludes that across localities, inflated transactions are more common for low-price properties and in low-income neighborhoods, presumably where financial constraints are more binding. The answer (a) is incorrect for two reasons. First, Ben-David (2011) never mentions anything about average-income homes, but rather solely focuses on low-income neighborhoods and secondly, he does not discuss any demographic evidence involving race. The answer (c) is incorrect because, once again, there is no discussion of high-income neighborhoods within the paper. Lastly, (d) is incorrect because the number of jobs worked by potential home buyers in low-income neighborhoods is not a factor cited by Ben-David (2011).

3. According the Ben-David (2011), all of the following are drivers of inflated transactions except:
   (a) Financing constraints on borrowers who have mortgages that are higher than 80 percent LTV

(b) The frequency of inflated transactions
(c) The role of intermediaries (real estate agents and mortgage brokers)
**(d) Unobserved variables, such as economic distress**
(e) All of the following are drivers of inflated transactions

**Explanation:** The correct answer is (d): Ben-David (2011) states specifically that it is unlikely that an unobservable variable drives the correlation between prices and the interaction between seller hints and high leverage. (a) Is a driver of inflated transactions as the amount of seller hints in transactions with buyer constraints increases from those who are not constrained borrower to those who have an LTV of 100 percent. (b) Is a driver as the number of inflated transactions increased as a percentage of all transactions from 2005 to 2008. Finally, (c) is a driver as Ben-David's (2011) study shows that in situations in which intermediaries have special stakes, seller hints are more prevalent.

## References

Aaron, B. (2006), "Interview with Kathy Coon", *Appraisal Buzz*, July.

Ben-David, I. (2011), "Financial constraints and inflated home prices during the real-estate boom", *American Economic Journal: Applied Economics* 3, 55–87.

Fannie Mae (2005), "Uniform Residential Appraisal Report." Form 1004.

Fannie Mae (2007), "Guide to Underwriting with DU."

Federal Housing Administration (2010), "FHA Announces Policy Changes to Address Risk and Strengthen Finances", *Press Release*, January 20.

Ho, Giang and A. Pennington-Cross (2007), "The varying effects of predatory lending laws on high-cost mortgage applications", *Federal Reserve Bank of St. Louis Review* 89, 39–59.

Hurst, E. and F. Stafford (2004), "Home Is Where the Equity Is: Mortgage Refinancing and Household Consumption", *Journal of Money, Credit, and Banking* 36, 985–1014.

Mian, A. and A. Sufi. (2009), "The Consequences of Mortgage Credit Expansion: Evidence from the U.S. Mortgage Default Crisis", *Quarterly Journal of Economics* 124, 1449–1496.

Mian, A. and A. Sufi (2014), *House of Debt*, USA: The University of Chicago Press.

Levitt, Steven D. and C. Syverson (2008), "Market Distortions When Agents Are Better Informed: The Value of Information in Real Estate Transactions", *Review of Economics and Statistics* 90, 599–611.

# Chapter 22
# Lending Standards

*In collaboration with* Allen Berman
and Connor Murphy

Las Vegas was the city of dreams, filled with luxurious casinos, restaurants, and an unparalleled nightlife. However, this life of paradise was only short lived when tough times came about the residents of Las Vegas. According to RealtyTrac, during the economic hardship of 2008, in the city of Las Vegas approximately 1 in every 13 homes were being foreclosed giving Las Vegas the highest foreclosure rate in any metropolitan city in the U.S. during this time period. Unfortunately, the real estate market business was struggling heavily, particularly American Invsco, a realtor company based out of Chicago. Invsco saw the opportunity of the housing bubble and capitalized on it by renovating approximately 678 condominiums. Due to the economic turmoil of 2008, it was confirmed that approximately 490 condominiums ended up being foreclosed. Before the housing downturn, Invsco encouraged many consumers to invest in real estate and supported using credit to invest beyond their means. Unfortunately for Invsco customers and many more, about a year and a half later their investment would be equal to $0, as Invsco was no longer making any profit. Why during this economic expansion were borrowers encouraged to take out loans they would not be able to pay off? How did this risky lending really come about and start to encourage borrowers into an endless cycle of debt?

The main goal of Dell'Ariccia, Igan, and Laevan (2012) is to connect the link between the decreased lending standards and the credit boom leading to the subprime mortgage crisis. They used denial rates and loan-to-income ratios as a measure of lending standards. To represent the credit expansion, the authors use the number of applications and the number of competing lenders. They also consider new entrants to the lending market and their effect on lending standards. They also explore how the securitization of loans led to riskier lending.

The data used to construct evidence showing the connection between the mortgage loan market and crash came from several sources. The main set of data came from economic and demographic information on applications straight from the mortgage loan. This data set came from the Home Mortgage Disclosure Act (HDMA) loan application registry. Other sources of data include the following: Loan Performance and the Federal Reserve Bank's Senior Loan Officer Opinion Survey. Additionally, there was a wide set of data available from the prime and subprime mortgage lenders, giving the authors the ability to proxy for the risk characteristics of loan applications and create more accurate data results across the two markets.

The primary economic model that Dell'Ariccia, Igan, and Laevan (2012) used was a linear regression model that allowed them to statistically analyze evidence behind decreased lending standards. The authors relied heavily on the denial rate as an indicating factor of lending standards at specific Metropolitan Statistical Area (MSA) levels. To ensure accuracy, the authors also used multiple control factors that were statistically proven to be a good indicator of loan denial rates. Some of these indicators were average income, income growth, unemployment rate, and self-employment rate. These indicators helped reduce confounding variables in the regression analysis giving the authors the most precise results.

This first main finding Dell'Ariccia, Igan, and Laevan (2012) expanded on is the relationship between the decrease in lending standards and the increase in housing prices. Given the authors had clear statistics to measure whether data came from the prime mortgage market or the subprime mortgage market, the first goal was aimed to exploit the decrease of lending standards in the subprime market. The first variable the authors analyzed to explain the decrease in lending standards was house prices. After the regression analysis, the authors concluded that a faster rate of house price is associated with lower denial rates. The negative association between denial rates and housing price growth was strongest in the subprime market, thus displaying that lenders were willing to gamble more on speculative borrowers in the subprime mortgage market.

The next main variable Dell'Ariccia, Igan, and Laevan (2012) explored was the relationship between denial rates and the number of loan applications. The authors explained how the number of loan applications is a variable that is nearly synonymous with a credit boom. The regression analysis findings for the relationship between number of loan applications and the denial rate were different for the subprime and prime markets. In the subprime market, a one standard deviation increase in the log of the number of applications reduced denial rates by 4 percentage points. In the prime market the relationship was positive, suggesting that an increase in the number of applications would increase the denial rate. These results led Dell'Ariccia, Igan, and Laevan (2012) to the important finding that there are different boom dynamics in the subprime and prime markets. To further emphasize this point, the authors explained that when using the number of competitors as the independent variable, they found that only the subprime market had a significant negative association between number of competitors and denial rate. This emphasized the idea that the subprime and prime markets have different dynamics affecting the decrease in lending standards.

Dell'Ariccia, Igan, and Laevan (2012) continued by looking at other dependent variables than denial rates. They turned to loan-to-income ratios to explain the movement of lending standards. The authors found that the results were very similar when using loan-to-income ratios in place of denial rates. For example, the authors found that there was a positive relationship between loan- to-income ratios and the number of applicants for a loan. This reinforced the idea that a decrease in lending standards leads to a credit boom.

Up until this point Dell'Ariccia, Igan, and Laevan (2012) had worked on comparing lending standards and credit booms, but they had not factored in the time or the size of the market or boom. The authors noticed that the relationship between the lending standards and booms became more strongly correlated across the spectrum of time of the data used. When controlling the variable of time, it was still found that lending standards are stronger when monetary policy is loose. The authors also looked at how the size of the market affected the relationship between the boom and lending standards. They found that the relationship was stronger as the population of the MSA increased. After considering the size of the market, they looked at how the size of the boom affected the relationship between the lending standards and credit boom. The authors looked at subsections of certain MSAs that had larger credit booms when compared to the other subsections and noticed that larger booms were correlated with stronger relationships between booms and standards.

Next, Dell'Ariccia, Igan, and Laevan (2012) explored how a changing market structure affected lending standards. They began by explaining how they would measure a change in market structure as the amount of market share controlled by new lenders varies. They used regression analysis to find the relationship between the amount of market share of new lenders and the denial rate of incumbent lenders. They found that both the subprime and prime market have a negative relationship between the two variables, with a stronger relationship being in the subprime market. These results suggested that incumbent lenders cut lending standards as more lenders enter the market. Also, the results further reinforce the idea that lending standards decreased in the subprime market during the credit boom.

Next, Dell'Ariccia, Igan, and Laevan (2012) analyzed how loan sales affected lending standards. They quantified mortgage securitization by tracking how many loans were sold within one year of origination. The amount of loan sales drastically increased within the period of focus (2000–2006). The authors accounted for this change by breaking the period in two and then calculating the relationship with the regression model. In the first period, an increase in loan sales led to a decrease in the denial rate for both the prime and subprime mortgage. In the second period, which is characterized by larger numbers of mortgage securitization, the decrease in denial rates in relation to an increase in loan sales was stronger than the previous period. In addition to analyzing the relationship between loan sales and denial rates, the authors looked at the relationship between loan sales and credit-to-income ratios. The credit-to-income ratio was a measure of credit market expansion. The regression model results show that as loan sales increase the credit-to-income also increases. Both of the relationships between loan sales and the two aforementioned dependent variables suggested that as mortgage securitization increases lenders are more encouraged to make riskier loans.

To further illustrate the decrease in lending standards, Dell'Ariccia, Igan, and Laevan (2012) focus on how monetary policy played a role in the subprime mortgage market compared to the prime mortgage market. In 2004 the U.S. started to increase interest rates and the denial rates of loans was predicted to follow because loan affordability goes down as interest rates rise. However, this was only the case in the prime mortgage market and not the subprime market. This trend of interest rates affecting the denial rate of only the prime mortgage market illustrates that loan affordability was only a factor in the prime mortgage market. The fact that loan affordability did not change the lending standards in the subprime market suggests that risky lending was prevalent in the subprime market during the credit boom.

In conclusion, Dell'Ariccia, Igan, and Laevan (2012) set out to find a relationship between credit booms and lending standards. They started by looking at four factors and analyzed how they interacted with lending standards. First, the authors found that lending standards decreased as housing prices rose. Second, they noticed that lending standards worsened as the credit boom became larger. Third, the authors found that the market structure had an effect on lending standards. For example, as new lenders entered the market lending standards became more relaxed. Finally, the authors found that mortgage securitization played a role in the changing of lending standards. They found that higher amounts of securitization led to decreasing lending standards. The authors used a variety of control variables to ensure that their findings were independent of confounding variables.

Some of the findings of Dell'Ariccia, Igan, and Laevan (2012) overlapped with the material in Mian and Sufi (2014). Both focused on the role of mortgage securitization in the subprime crisis. They both came to the conclusion that mortgage securitization led to riskier lending. Mian and Sufi (2014) went into further detail describing how securitization led to risky lending. They explained that banks were eager to create more mortgage-backed securities (MBS) and because of this they were more inclined to lend to marginal borrowers.

After reviewing Dell'Ariccia, Igan, and Laevan (2012), there were some possible problems. The paper used its findings to make conclusions without explaining how it used the empirical evidence to make the specific conclusion. They could improve their paper by explaining how the findings were interrelated to give the reader a more holistic understanding of the material presented.

Suggestions for further investigation is to look at how monetary policy affects lending standards. This would allow Dell'Ariccia, Igan, and Laevan (2012) to look into how the monetary policy created the subprime crisis or how it failed to prevent the crisis. After completing this research, researchers can form opinions on how one should utilize monetary policy to prevent another subprime crisis.

## Multiple Choice Questions

1. According to Dell'Ariccia, Igan, and Laevan (2012), which of the following statements accurately describes why the increased rate of housing price appreciation resulted in the lowering of denial rates?
   (a) Lenders were gambling on speculative borrowers
   (b) The positive effect of borrower's higher net worth on creditworthiness

(c) Higher housing prices led to a decrease in the risk of mortgage backed securities

(d) **(a) and (b)**

**Explanation:** (a) is correct because the research paper explains that lenders were gambling that housing prices would continue to increase. The potential risk of default of the speculative borrowers would be outweighed by the additional profits of an increase of loans if the housing market continued to increase. (b) is correct because as net worth of borrowers increase the default risk that the lender must bear decreases. This means that a larger proportion of borrowers seeking a loan now qualify for loans, which leads to lower denial rates.

2. According to Dell'Ariccia, Igan, and Laevan (2012), which of the following does not lead to a decrease in the denial rate of loans in the subprime market?

(a) The amount of securitization of mortgages increases

(b) The amount of loan applications increases

(c) **The loan-to-income ratio increases**

(d) The income of potential borrowers increases

**Explanation:** (c) is correct because the loan-to-income ratio is another measure of borrowing standards. If the borrowing standard of denial rate goes down, then the borrowing standard of loan-to-income should loosen as well. This would mean that the ratio decreases. Some people may think that option (b) is also correct, but it is not because of the distinction between the subprime market and the prime market. In the subprime market as loan applications increases the denial rate does decrease. If we were talking about the prime market, option (b) would be correct because as loan application increases denial rates do increase.

3. According to Dell'Ariccia, Igan, and Laevan (2012), which of the following is a true example of how market structure changes denial rates?

(a) **As more lenders entered the market, denial rates decreased**

(b) As more lenders entered the market, denial rates increased

> (c) High denial rates of incumbent lenders attracted more lenders to the market
>
> (d) Low denial rates of incumbent lenders attracted more lenders to the market

**Explanation:** (a) is correct. According to Dell'Ariccia, Igan, and Laevan (2012), incumbent lenders cut lending standards as entrants to the market increase. (c) and (d) discuss how the denial rates of incumbent lenders will attract or prevent new entrants to the market. These options are incorrect because it was found that the current denial rates of incumbent lenders have little to no correlation to the amount of new lenders that will enter the loan market.

## References

G. Dell'Ariccia, D. Igan and L. Laeven (2012), "Credit Booms and Lending Standards: Evidence from the Subprime Mortgage Market," *Journal of Money, Credit and Banking* 44, 367–384.

Gillette, F. (2013), "After Las Vegas's Housing Crash, Fraud, Ferraris, and Gun Fights", Bloomberg, September 12.

Mian, A. and A. Sufi (2014), *House of Debt*, USA: The University of Chicago Press.

# Chapter 23
# Lax Screening

*In collaboration with* Daniel Fisher
and Jaron Kleiman

The housing bubble that preceded the Great Recession had many underlying causes. One of the key causes of this bubble was the ease in which individuals were being granted mortgage loans. This credit expansion effectively granted loans to individuals who would have otherwise not been able to meet the necessary criterion. Was this decline in lending standards the root cause for the housing bubble?

The Great Recession devastated the United States during the late 2000s and its source can be contributed to multiple, interrelated factors, as the overall economy works as a singular engine. The securitized, subprime mortgage industry, however, played a substantial role in the financial crisis as the extraordinary amount of debt issued to homeowners could not be sustained. To understand this principal contributor of the financial crisis, one must analyze why the subprime mortgage market had a severe impact on the economy, and whether or not securitization had a detrimental effect on the *ex-ante* screening efforts of loan originators.

Keys *et al.* (2010) evaluated data on subprime mortgage securities and their impact on the financial crisis. They investigated whether or not the securitization market of the early 2000s incentivized unregulated, public companies to relax their screening standards on mortgage borrowers categorized as "subprime." By doing so, such careless underwriting efforts were argued to have caused the collapse of the economy.

To determine the primary cause of the financial crisis, it is important to examine the securitized subprime mortgage market. In general, securitization of debt improves efficiency, shares risks as well as reduces cost of capital for banks. Due to these benefits, the intermediaries originating the illiquid subprime mortgages utilized a negligent standard of screening. Keys *et al.* (2010) indicated that the intermediaries' framework of "originate-to-distribute" contrasts from the "originate-to-own" model primarily because it misaligns incentives when evaluating borrowers. Because of this misalignment, the intermediaries' process was scrutinized because of a decreased incentive to mitigate risk as they passed it to investors. The screening heavily emphasized a threshold for loans to be securitized, particularly relying on FICO scores. The FICO score of 620 stood as this threshold, where scores above 620 were more easily securitized and scores below 620 required additional investigation of the creditworthiness of the borrower. Concern emerged as loans that fell slightly above and below this threshold showed measurable differences for how they were evaluated by lenders and in performance of the borrower. Keys *et al.* (2010) pointed out that the loans that indicated a borrower Fair Isaac Corporation (FICO) score slightly over 620, (i.e. 621–625), were experiencing default at a significantly greater rate than those moderately below 620 (i.e. 615–619). A suspect to this abnormality rests on the screening standards that were employed by the intermediaries as hard information, such as the FICO score, became the leading factor for decision making.

Keys *et al.* (2010) utilized data from Loan Performance, the sole resource for in-depth information about the non-agency security markets, to analyze the subprime mortgage market. As of December 2006, there were over 8,000 home equity and non-prime mortgage pools, which included 16.5 million loans with over $1.6 trillion in outstanding loan balances. The data from loan performance covered 90 percent of the securitized, subprime loans in the market and supplied users with variables from standard loan applications including loan amounts, terms, loan-to-value (LTV) ratios, credit scores, and interest rate types. The subprime securitization primarily focused on the creditworthiness of a borrower, reflected in the individual's FICO score. However, the fatal flaw with relying on a FICO score is that it only quantifies the probability of a borrower experiencing a negative credit event in the subsequent two years, thus failing to examine the future income and assets of the borrower. Due to mortgage lenders' concern with long-term credit risk, most lenders required extensive documentation from the borrower to gauge their creditworthiness for the originate-to-hold model. However, for the originate-to-sell model, lenders may loosen measures in assembling their analysis, as they distribute the loans and do not hold the default risk.

When borrowers applied for loans, the type of documentation they provided falls into two classifications. The first is hard information, which includes background material provided in the borrower's loan application and reports from credit bureaus, particularly the FICO credit report. Second is soft information, which is more challenging to summarize as it includes income stability, assets owned, and other information that is timely and costly to collect. Loans can also be categorized into how much information is given. The data utilized have three levels of documentation: full documentation that reports both income and assets, limited documentation that includes assets and excludes income, and no documentation that omits both income and assets. Keys *et al.* (2010) research combines low and no documentation into "low documentation" category. Distinction between the type of information as well as the level of information is significant throughout their article.

Securitization begins with packaging accepted loans into pools and then selling rights to benefit from pools are evaluated by investors based on FICO scores, LTV ratios, interest rates, and ratings given by rating agencies. Keys *et al.* (2010) research focuses on FICO scores as the fundamental criteria for lenders' evaluation of loans. The "Rule of Thumb" of accepting loans with borrowers'

FICO scores of 620 or greater was originally set by GSEs, Freddie and Fannie, when introducing securitization of loans in the 1970s. As the role shifted to companies such as investment banks and hedge funds who conduct private label securitization (PLS), Keys *et al.* (2010) found evidence that adherence to this cut off because of mortgage-backed security (MBS) investors increased demand for securitized loans.

The fundamental problem arose when investors based decisions on solely hard information. This occurred for FICO scores just above 620, compared to below 620 scores, which were still being evaluated on both hard and soft information. If lenders were screened similarly for the 620 thresholds, there should not be any observable difference in default rates among these loans. However, if there is a difference, it is believed to be due to securitization and the originate-to-distribute model that increased substantially prior to the financial crisis.

Results of Keys *et al.* (2010) research uncovered three significant findings. First, there was a significant difference in risk mitigation between Government Sponsored Enterprises (GSE) securitization and PLS. From 2001 to 2005, PLS market acceptance growth for full documentation for mortgage loans was 445 percent while acceptance growth for limited documentation loans was 972 percent and less hard information in the form of low documentation borrowers. They also found less equity in these loans, or higher LTV ratios, which entails more risk, yet no difference in interest rates to compensate investors.

Second, Keys *et al.* (2010) discovered that the performance of loans with higher credit scores defaulted more often than lower credit loans in the post-2000 period, especially the loans originated in 2005. The data show that defaults began 4 months to 24 months after origination and, on average, loans that are just below 620 FICO scores are 20 percent less likely to default after a year compared to just above 620. Overall, loans with higher credit scores performed worse around the 620 threshold.

Finally, they found variation from a natural experiment in which two states enforced anti-predatory lending laws. In 2002, both Georgia and New Jersey enacted anti-predatory to protect mortgage borrowers. Keys *et al.* (2010) explains if lenders used the 620 FICO score as an optimal cut-off for screening unrelated to securitization, passage of these laws would not affect the screening standards around the threshold. However, after enactment loans around the 620 FICO score threshold fell by 95 percent and default rates of loans just above the 620 threshold were less than default rates below the 620 threshold, only when the law was in effect.

Conclusions in Keys *et al.* (2010) indicated about 10–25 percent increase, on average, in defaults by doubling the amount of loans securitized from 2000 to 2006 as well as a causal link that the ease of securitization decreased incentives to screen borrowers thoroughly. Also, the authors confirmed that anti-predatory laws changed lender behavior in the subprime market, based on ease of securitization, which suggests that while the laws were in effect, significantly less subprime mortgages were securitized which forced originators to hold the risk. Keys *et al.* (2010) explains that if lenders were holding optimal levels of risk where it was easier to securitize, there should not have been a difference in defaults around the 620 FICO score threshold.

Securitization offers benefits of improving efficiency in credit markets and diversifying risk. However, the underlying assumption indicates that no information, such as borrower credit quality, is lost in transition when the distance increases between holders of debt and borrowers. Ultimately, results found that the originate-to-distribute model of securitization does not leave lenders with enough skin in the game to lend responsibly without regulation.

Congruent with Keys *et al.* (2010) research, Mian and Sufi (2014) acknowledge the positive correlation between increases of loans in low-credit quality ZIP codes with the increase in PLS, suggesting that incentives to relax screening standards may have existed. Mian and Sufi (2014) theorize that investors underestimated the default probability and the correlation of loans packaged in subprime MBS, and because of this, these assets were perceived and rated as very safe to hold. They also suggest that banks took advantage of investors' mistakes and were incentivized to decrease screening standards, and disguise the real vulnerabilities and risks of these assets for profits. Testing their theory, Mian and Sufi (2014) directly cite Keys *et al.* (2010) research regarding the 620 FICO score threshold and concur that if lending standards were consistent, all mortgages to borrowers with a score around 620 should have roughly the same default rates. However, Mian and Sufi highlight that Keys *et al.* (2010) results showed the opposite as there was a discontinuous jump at the 620 threshold.

Examining what kind of mortgages are susceptible to originator misbehavior, Mian and Sufi (2014) concluded that low documentation mortgages where borrowers did not provide information about income, or other soft information were most vulnerable. During this period, banks were much less careful about investigating low-documentation borrowers when they met the 620 threshold to be securitized, which essentially lowered the incentives of banks to screen and monitor borrowers.

In addition, Mian and Sufi (2014) suggested that investors were deceived to take on more risk without fair compensation, along with the rating agencies ignoring obvious information, such as FICO scores, LTV ratios, when assigning ratings to private label MBS. Mian and Sufi (2014) also draw conclusions from research conducted by Demyanyk and Van Hemert (2011), who identified that the decline of loan quality was evident as the average LTV ratio increased, the fraction of limited documentation loans increased, and the subprime–prime rate spread decreased. Essentially, after lenders flooded the market with poor credit quality loans, investors fueled the oversupply of credit by making simple mistakes in models when assessing risks associated with MBS. In turn, the intermediaries packaging the loans exploited these mistakes made by investors.

Although Keys *et al.* research provides a general understanding of what was occurring in the securitized market, the whole mortgage market is not represented in this data. The non-securitized loans also need to be understood as banks used the 620 threshold to originate non-securitized mortgages as well. The metric may not be the number of securitized loans originated, but rather the chance that a loan is securitized. The change in standards not only affected the number of loans securitized, but also the number of loans that the banks originated. Thus, the securitization rate could be a better measure of describing default as banks also lessened their standards for underwriting.

Research conducted by Bubb and Kaufman (2011) for the Federal Reserve pinpoints the reaction of the securitization rate to the uptick of the defaults at 620. It was found that an increase in the lending rate contributes to the increase in securitized loans, but there is no increase in the securitization rate. Due to this discovery, it is difficult to conclude that the increase in defaults was attributable to banks relaxing their screening standards.

Another factor that contradicts the position that FICO scores at the 620 threshold defaulted due to lax underwriting involves credit cut-off standards that Freddie Mac and Fannie Mae used as a rule of thumb. The government-sponsored enterprises mandated the use of a 620 FICO score as a screening standard, but this does not explain which defaults were due to securitization and which contributed to the rule of thumb of the lender. Based on the layers involved — from the banks to the intermediaries and the intermediaries to the investors — an argument can be made that the defaults are not caused by the lenient standards of underwriting using a 620 FICO score threshold.

Areas that could be further investigated in the realm of the securitized market include the process for underwriting prime loans, the loan documentation standards the threshold applied to, and the assumptions used to draw their conclusions. The screening standards used in the overall market could be looked into and determined the qualities that matter most to the underwriters and a comparison could be drawn between the prime and subprime loans. Loan documentation goes hand in hand with the process, and a more rigorous process would yield additional documentation. Research into the documentation could further enhance the understanding of the securitization process. Lastly, if assumptions would be changed, such that there are loans that have the possibility of either being securitized or purchased by government-sponsored entities, different results could be attained and provide better insight on the relationship between securitization and lax screening practices. By furthering the research on the securitization market, the factors affecting default can be understood more completely.

## Multiple Choice Questions

1. According to Keys *et al.* (2010), on average, loans that are just below 620 FICO scores were ____ likely to default after a year compared to just above 620.

    (a) 4 percent less
    (b) 10 percent more
    **(c) 20 percent less**
    (d) 24 percent more
    (e) None of the above

**Explanation**: Keys *et al.* (2010) discovered that the performance of loans with higher credit scores defaulted more often than lower credit loans in the post-2000 period, especially the loans originated in 2005. The data show that defaults began 4 months to 24 months after origination and, on average, loans that are just below 620 FICO scores are 20 percent less likely to default after a year compared to just above 620. Overall, loans with higher credit scores perform worse around the 620 threshold.

2. The natural experiment regarding anti-predatory lending laws discussed by Keys *et al.* (2010) is significant because:

    (a) PLS started securitizing more, therefore earning more than GSE securitization
    (b) Lender behavior altered dramatically after the laws were passed
    (c) Loans around the threshold fell while these laws were in place
    **(d) (b) and (c)**
    (e) All of the above

**Explanation**: If lenders used the 620 FICO score as an optimal cut-off for screening unrelated to securitization, passage of these laws would not affect the screening standards around the threshold. However, loans around the threshold fell by 95 percent while these laws were in place.

3. According to Mian and Sufi (2014), what kind of mortgages are susceptible to originator misbehavior?

   **(a) Low documentation mortgages where borrowers did not provide information about income, or soft information**
   (b) Borrowers whose FICO scores were just above the 620 score threshold
   (c) Borrowers whose FICO scores were just below the 620 score threshold
   (d) Those in low-credit quality ZIP codes, with high LTV ratios

**Explanation**: During this period, banks were much less careful about investigating low-documentation borrowers when they met the 620 threshold to be securitized, which essentially lowered the incentives of banks to screen and monitor borrowers.

## References

Bubb, R. and A. Kaufman (2011), "The Uncertain Case Against Mortgage Securitization," *Federal Reserve Bank of Atlanta*, Real Estate Research.

Keys, B., T. Mukherjee, A. Seru and V. Vig (2010), "Did Securitization Lead to Lax Screening? Evidence From Subprime Loans", *The Quarterly Journal of Economics* 125, 307–362.

Mian, A. and A. Sufi (2014), *House of Debt*, USA: The University of Chicago Press.

Yuliya, D. and O. Van Hemert (2011), "Understanding the Subprime Mortgage Crisis", *Review of Financial Studies* 24, 1848–1880.

# Bibliography

Aaron, B. (2006), "Interview with Kathy Coon", *Appraisal Buzz*, July.

Agarwal, S., B. W. Ambrose, S. Chomsisengphet and A. B. Sanders (2012), "Thy Neighbor's Mortgage: Does Living in a Subprime Neighborhood Affect One's Probability of Default?", *Real Estate Economics* 40, 1–22.

Annenberg, E. and E. Kung (2014), "Estimates of the Size and Source of Price Declines Due to Nearby Foreclosures", *American Economic Review* 104, 2527–2551.

Bailey, M. J., R. F. Muth and H. O. Nourse (1963), "A Regression Model for Real Estate Price Index Construction", *Journal of the American Statistical Association* 58, 933–942.

Ben-David, I. (2011), "Financial Constraints and Inflated Home Prices During the Real-Estate Boom", *American Economic Journal: Applied Economics* 3, 55–87.

Bhutta, N. (2014), "GSE Activity and Mortgage Supply in Lower-Income and Minority Neighborhoods: The Effect of the Affordable Housing Goals", *Journal of Real Estate Finance and Ecomomics* 45, 238–261.

Bolotnyy, V. (2014), "The Government-Sponsored Enterprises and the Mortgage Crisis: The Role of the Affordable Housing Goals", *Real Estate Economics* 42, 724–755.

Brevoort, K. P. and C. R. Cooper (2013), "Foreclosure's Wake: The Credit Experiences of Individuals Following Foreclosure", *Real Estate Economics* 41, 747–792.

Bubb, R. and A. Kaufman (2011), "The Uncertain Case Against Mortgage Securitization," *Federal Reserve Bank of Atlanta*, Real Estate Research.

Campbell, J., S. Giglio, and P. Pathak (2011) "Forced Sales and House Prices", *American Economic Review* 101, 2108–2131.

Demyanyk, Y. and O. Van Hermert (2011), "Understanding the Subprime Mortgage Crisis", *The Review of Financial Studies* 24, 1848–1880.

Fannie Mae (2005), "Uniform Residential Appraisal Report", Form 1004.

Fannie Mae (2007), "Guide to Underwriting with DU." https://www.fanniemae.com

Federal Housing Administration (2010), "FHA Announces Policy Changes to Address Risk and Strengthen Finances", *Press Release*, January 20.

G. Dell'Ariccia, D. Igan and L. Laeven (2012), "Credit Booms and Lending Standards: Evidence from the Subprime Mortgage Market", *Journal of Money, Credit and Banking* 44, 367–384.

Gabriel, S. and S. Rosenthal (2010), "Do the GSEs Expand the Supply of Mortgage Credit? New Evidence of Crowd Out in the Secondary Mortgage Market", *Journal of Public Economics* 94, 975–986.

Gabriel, S. A. and S. Rosenthal (2015), "The Boom, the Bust and the Future of Homeownership", *Real Estate Economics* 43, 334–374.

Gerardi, K., Lehnert, A., Sherlund, S. and P. Willen (2010), "Making Sense of the Subprime Crisis", *Brookings Papers on Economic Activity* 39, 69–159.

Gillette, F. (2013) "After Las Vegas's Housing Crash, Fraud, Ferraris, and Gun Fights", Bloomberg, September 12.

Hancock, D. and W. Passmore (2011), "Did the Federal Reserve's MBS Purchase Program Lower Mortgage Rates?", *Journal of Monetary Economics* 58, 498–514.

Harding, J. P., E. Rosenblatt and V. W. Yao (2009), "The Contagion Effect of Foreclosed Properties", *Journal of Urban Economics* 66, 164–178.

Hartley, D. (2014), "The Effect of Foreclosures on Nearby Housing Prices: Supply or Dis-Amenity?", *Regional Science and Urban Economics* 49, 108–117.

Henderson, J. V. and Y. M. Ioannides (1983), "A Model of Housing Tenure Choice", *American Economic Review* 73, 98–113.

Ho, Giang and A. Pennington-Cross (2007), "The Varying Effects of Predatory Lending Laws on High-Cost Mortgage Applications", *Federal Reserve Bank of St. Louis Review* 89, 39–59.

Holden S., A. Kelly, D. McManus, T. Scharlemann, R. Singer and J. Worth (2012), "The HAMP NPV Model: Development and Early Performance", *Real Estate Economics* 40, S32–S64.

Hollifield, B. (2011), "Comments on 'Did the Federal Reserve's MBS Purchase Program Lower Mortgage Rates?'", *Journal of Monetary Economics* 58, 515–517.

Hurst, E. and F. Stafford (2004), "Home Is Where the Equity Is: Mortgage Refinancing and Household Consumption", *Journal of Money, Credit, and Banking* 36, 985–1014.

Jickling, M. (2008), *Fannie Mae and Freddie Mac in Conservatorship*, Congressional Research Service, Library of Congress.

Keys, B., T. Mukherjee, A. Seru and V. Vig (2010), "Did Securitization Lead to Lax Screening? Evidence from Subprime Loans", *The Quarterly Journal of Economics* 125, 307–362.

Levitt, S. D., and C. Syverson (2008), "Market Distortions When Agents Are Better Informed: The Value of Information in Real Estate Transactions", *Review of Economics and Statistics* 90, 599–611.

Lewis, M. (2010), *The Big Short: Inside the Doomsday Machine*, W. W. Norton.

Luque, J. (2015), *Urban Land Economics*, Springer International Publishing.

Luque, J. and T. Riddiough (2016), "The credit scoring channel in the sub-prime conduit mortgage market", mimeo.

Mian, A. and A. Sufi (2009), "The Consequences of Mortgage Credit Expansion: Evidence from the U.S. Mortgage Default Crisis", *Quarterly Journal of Economics* 124, 1449–1496.

Mian, A. and A. Sufi (2011), "House Prices, Home Equity Borrowing, and the US Household Leverage Crisis", *American Economic Review* 101, 2132–2156.

Mian A. and A. Sufi (2014), *House of Debt*, USA: The University of Chicago Press.

Mian, A. and A. Sufi (2015), *House of Debt*, USA: The University of Chicago Press.

Mian, A., A. Sufi and F. Trebbi (2010), "The Political Economy of the US Mortgage Default Crisis", *American Economic Review* 100, 1967–1998.

Mian, A., A. Sufi and F. Trebbi (2012), "Foreclosures, House Prices, and the Real Economy", *The Nation Bureau of Economic Research* NBER Working Paper No. 16685.

Mian, A., A. Sufi and F. Trebbi (2013), "The Political Economy of the Subprime Mortgage Credit Expansion", *Quarterly Journal of Political Science* 8, 373–408.

Mian, A., K. Rao and A. Sufi (2013), "Household Balance Sheets, Consumption, and the Economic Slump", *Quarterly Journal of Economics* 128, 1687–1726.

Molloy, R. and H. Shan (2011), "The Post-foreclosure Experience of U.S. Households", *Federal Reserve Board of Governors*, May.

Molloy R. and H. Shan (2013), "The Post-foreclosure Experience of U.S. Households", *Real Estate Economics* 41(2), 225–254.

Stroebel, J. C. and J. B. Taylor (2012), "Estimated Impact of the Fed's Mortgage-Backed Securities Purchase Program", *International Journal of Central Banking* 8, 1–42.

Sun, L., S. Titman and G. Twite (2015), "REIT and Commercial Real Estate Returns: A Postmortem of the Financial Crisis", *Real Estate Economics* 43, 8–36.

Yuliya, D. and O. Van Hemert (2011), "Understanding the Subprime Mortgage Crisis", *Review of Financial Studies* 24, 1848–1880.

# Index